This for That

◆

A treasury of savvy substitutions for the creative cook

◆

Created, Tested and Written by
Meryl Nelson

Published by
R&E Publishers
Post Office Box 2008
Saratoga, California 95070-2008
Phone (408) 866-6303
Fax (408) 866-0825

Fax, Phone and Written Orders Welcome

This for That
Revised, expanded, third edition
Published October 1990
ISBN 0-88247-847-6
LC No. 90-62126

Helped and Encouraged by
Frances Thoman
(My Mom)

Edited by
Shirley Sing
(My Super Friend)

Illustrated by
Lyndee L. Sing
(My Super Friend's Daughter)

Dedicated to
Bob, Liz, Alan and John
(My Cheering Section

When you're out of ...

When you're out of ...

When you're out of ...

When you're out of ...

Before you begin ...

Welcome to the revised and expanded third edition of the THIS FOR THAT Cookbook. Retaining all the straight substitutions, alternate recipes and helpful hints of the second edition — our new version enters the new decade with some microwave conversions as well as Micro Facts and Hints, starting on page 86.

Only those recipes in which microwave cooking saved time or effort were converted. You'll see **Micro**≈ under these, and they are starred in the Index. Candies and jams do well in the microwave, but you are safer using specifically developed recipes rather than conversions.

CAUTION: always use microwave safe utensils. Check the instruction book that came with your oven for safety precautions. Our recipes presume **that all utensils mentioned are microwave proof.**

Unless otherwise noted, all recipes are cooked on High Power. Microwaves vary in number of watts, so check your manual or oven (usually on the back). Our directions are for 600-650 watts, so if yours is less — increase the time 20 to 30 seconds per minute. Less standing time is required.

If you successfully microwave one of the recipes in this book that we haven't done — please send us your directions — making sure to indicate any changes of ingredient amounts as well as cooking time and power used. More about this on page 101.

While none of the recipes was written specifically for people on special diets or those with allergies; responses from readers of earlier editions indicated that some hints and recipes were especially helpful. Look for recipes with the symbols listed below, and for the "Special Recipe Index" on pages 96 and 97.

A▶	Allergy
LC▶	Low Calorie
LF▶	Low Fat
AP▶	Alternative Protein
SS▶	Sugar Substitute

Our thanks to Martha Costick, M.P.H., R.D., former Public Health Nutritionist of Amador and Calaveras Counties, California. She provided data for the alternative protein information on page 51 and checked the special recipes marked with the symbols shown above.

When you're out of ...

ABALONE

Hungry for abalone, but the price is sky-high, and no chance to catch any? Here's a tasty taste-alike.

MAKE-BELIEVE ABALONE

4 halves boned chicken breasts (1/2 breast per person)
1 can (15 oz.) minced clams   1 clove garlic, minced

Pound raw chicken breasts until about 1/4 inch thick. (You can cut the breasts from two whole chickens and save the rest for another meal.) Soak the chicken breasts in the juice drained from the canned clams — bottled clam juice does not have an intense enough flavor. Add the garlic and soak for 36 to 48 hours. Turn the breasts once or twice to make sure all parts are permeated with clam juice.

When ready to serve, drain; then dip in egg and fine bread crumbs and fry quickly in a small amount of oil over moderately high heat until the crust is brown and the chicken done. This takes about 5 minutes.

AFTER-DINNER MINTS

Made just like taffy, these refreshing mints are fun to make, and change from a hard, chewy consistency into a melt-in-the-mouth texture after a sugaring-off process.

MELT-AWAY MINTS

3 c sugar   1/2 t cream of tartar
1 1/4 c water   15 drops oil of peppermint

Thoroughly combine first three ingredients in saucepan. Cook to hard ball stage (260°). Pour into lightly buttered shallow pan and let stand undisturbed until cool enough to handle.

Have peppermint ready to add during the first few minutes of pulling. Butter hands lightly. Pull candy. (Stretch, fold over, stretch — repeating until candy has a satinlike finish and is quite elastic with a series of parallel groves on the surface.)

Pull candy into 1/2-inch rope; then cut with scissors into 1/4 to 1/2-inch lengths. Drop pieces into pan of powdered sugar, coating well, and keeping each piece separate.

Cover pan and let candy crystallize for 24 to 36 hours. Place sugar and candy into sieve to shake out excess sugar. Store candy in airtight container. These mints will keep indefinitely. Makes 1 1/4 lbs.

When you're out of ...

APPLES

When your garden produces zucchini instead of apples, you can get rid of 2 large zucchini (or two quarts) in this

APPLELESS APPLE CRUNCH

First, change your zucchini into apples
2 large zucchini (2 quarts peeled and sliced)
2/3 c lemon juice   1/4 t nutmeg
1 c sugar   1/2 t cinnamon

Peel and remove seeds and pulp from zucchini; then slice, and cut the slices into quarters. Simmer, covered, in lemon juice until zucchini is crisp-tender. Add sugar and spices, and simmer a few minutes more.
Next, make the pastry.

4 c flour   2 c sugar
1/2 t salt   1 c margarine

Mix all ingredients with a pastry blender. Reserve one cup flour mixture for topping, adding 1 teaspoon cinnamon. Remove another 1/2 cup of flour mixture and add to cooked squash.
Place remaining pastry mix on a greased cookie sheet, or jelly roll pan, pressing down firmly. Bake 10 minutes at 375°. Remove from oven and spread zucchini over it. Sprinkle on topping and bake for 30 minutes at 375°, or until light brown.

OR:
If you still have some large zucchini — try a pie. Make "apple" slices as for "Apple Crunch" above.

ZUCCHINI "APPLE" PIE

5 c zucchini pieces   1/8 t salt
1 1/4 t sugar   2 T flour
1 1/2 t cream of tartar   1/2 t nutmeg
2 T lemon juice   1 1/2 t cinnamon
          Pastry for a two crust pie

Combine ingredients. Put in unbaked shell. Cover with top crust. Bake at 400° for 45-50 minutes.
Here's a neat trick. Instead of using water to seal top and bottom crusts together, rub edge of bottom crust with an ice cube; put on top crust and crimp edges.

OR:
Try this apple-less version. No one will believe you were actually out of apples.

MOCK APPLE PIE INSTEAD

14 soda crackers	1 1/2 t cream of tartar
1 1/2 c water	1 t cinnamon
1 1/4 c sugar	2 t butter or margarine

Break crackers in fourths into unbaked pie shell. Mix rest of ingredients and bring to boil. Pour over crackers. Cover with top crust, or crumb topping and bake at 375° for 45 minutes. No one will believe you were actually out of apples!

APPLESAUCE, FOR CAKES OR COOKIES

Use your ingenuity. Try mashed pears (add a pinch of ginger), apricots (nutmeg goes well), or any other fruit you can "sauce" to substitute for the applesauce called for in your recipe.

OR:
If you have some applesauce, but not quite enough — you can fill up your short measure with almost anything you can mash. Doesn't have to be fruit; mashed potatoes or squash works equally well.

ARTICHOKE HEARTS, MARINATED

Use brussel sprouts — naturally not the same flavor, but adds a leafy surprise to your tossed green salad.

About 12 brussel sprouts — fresh or frozen, cooked just crisp-tender.

1/2 c oil	1/3 c vinegar	1 clove garlic, crushed

Cut cooked brussel sprouts in half and put in a pint jar. Mix oil, vinegar and garlic and pour over sprouts. Marinate 24 hours (at least). Shake the jar once in awhile.

When you're out of ...

ASCORBIC ACID

If you have none of that handy powder to keep fruit from darkening while frozen, and a lug of peaches to freeze — mix 1 can (6 oz.) of frozen orange juice concentrate (undiluted) with 6 cups of sugar. Slice 30 peaches into the mixture and let marinate for an hour or so. Place in containers and freeze.

OR:

For canning or freezing any kind of fruit that you want to keep from darkening while you're peeling and preparing — put the prepared fruit into two quarts of water with the juice of 1/2 lemon.

OR:

No lemons? If you have some Vitamin C tablets handy (it is ascorbic acid), try this:

Dissolve one tablet (1000 mg) of Vitamin C in two quarts of water. (Crushing the tablet between two tablespoons reduces the dissolving time.) You will notice a white residue which will not dissolve, but that is merely harmless, tasteless, inert material put in to hold the tablets together.

When you're out of ...

BAKING POWDER

Try this homemade mix. It works!

Mix

| 2 T cream of tartar | 1 T baking soda | 1 T cornstarch |

Use same measurements as the commercial mix.

When you're out of ...

BAKING POWDER AND EGGS

When you're out of both baking powder and eggs, here are two good cakes to try. Both are light, moist and keep well.

A▶   BLACK DEVIL'S *GOOD* CAKE

2 c flour	1 T baking soda
1 3/4 c sugar	2/3 c oil
1/2 c cocoa	1 c buttermilk
1/2 t salt	1 c strong coffee

Sift together flour, sugar, cocoa, salt and soda. Add oil and milk. Stir until well-blended. Bring coffee to a boil and stir gently into batter. (Mixture will be "soupy".) Pour into greased and floured 9x13-inch pan. Bake at 350° oven for 35 to 40 minutes.

A▶   BUTTERMILK CHOCOLATE CAKE

Do not use a mixer on this one.

2 c sugar	2 t salt
3 c flour	1 c oil
2 t baking soda	3 c buttermilk
1/2 c plus 2 T cocoa	4 t vanilla

Sift dry ingredients together; then stir in remaining ingredients. Bake in greased and floured 9x13-inch pan about 40 minutes in 350° oven.

When you're out of ...

BAKING POWDER, EGGS AND MILK

Here are three recipes that go one step further — none of them requires milk, and all are delicious. Crazy Cake (sometimes called "Wacky Cake") was born during the Depression and is still a favorite. The original version lets you mix the dry ingredients right in the pan you're going to bake it in; however, you can be more conventional and put everything into a mixer bowl and blend that way.

A▶   ORIGINAL CRAZY CAKE

3 c flour	2 T vinegar
2 c sugar	2 t vanilla
2 t baking soda	2/3 c oil
1 t salt	2 c cold water
6 T cocoa	

Mix dry ingredients together in a greased 9x13-inch pan. Make three "holes" in this mixture. Pour oil in one hole, vinegar in another and vanilla in the third. Pour water over all and mix well with a fork. Bake at 350° for 30 minutes.

Micro≈ Halve the recipe. Mix as directed in an 8 or 9-inch micro-proof pan. Micro on high for 6-7 minutes. Rotate 1/4 turn twice, if you have no turntable. Test: pick inserted near center comes clean. Place dish on flat heat-proof surface for 10 minutes to finish cooking, then on wire rack. Cut when cool.

OR:

Don't let the vinegar scare you — these cookies are light, crisp and tasty with no hint of what makes them that way. They are done when a light golden brown.

A▶   SUGAR CRISPIES

1/2 c margarine, softened	1 3/4 c flour
3/4 c sugar	2 t vinegar
1 t baking soda	1 t vanilla

Cream the margarine and sugar together. Sift together flour and baking soda and add to creamed mixture. Stir in vinegar and vanilla. Drop from a teaspoon onto ungreased cookie sheet. Bake 12-15 minutes at 350°. Makes 5 dozen.

OR:

Save those expensive potato chips that got smashed in the bottom of the bag in this unusual cookie recipe when you're out of baking powder, eggs and milk.

A▶   POTATO CHIP COOKIES

3/4 c margarine	1/2 c crushed potato chips
1/2 c sugar	1/2 c nuts, chopped
1 1/2 c sifted flour	1 t vanilla

Cream together margarine and sugar. Add sifted flour, chips and nuts. Stir in vanilla.

Drop from teaspoon onto ungreased cookie sheets and bake at 350° for about 15 minutes. Makes 3 dozen cookies.

BAKING POWDER, MILK AND SHORTENING

This easy-to-make cake is good for breakfast, warm; and great, when cool, for lunch or dinner dessert. Can be dressed up with a spoonful of whipped topping.

LF▶   FRUIT COCKTAIL CAKE

1 1/2 c sugar	1/4 t salt
2 c flour	2 eggs, well beaten
2 t soda	1 can (16 oz.) fruit cocktail

Sift dry ingredients together. Add beaten eggs and 1 can (16 oz.) fruit cocktail (not drained). Mix well and pour into a 9x13-inch pan, greased and floured. Bake at 325° for 40 to 60 minutes.

When you're out of ...

BARBECUE SAUCE

All set to brush some canned, sliced ham-pork product with barbecue sauce, and find an empty bottle? Try using some bottled Russian dressing (or even French or Italian) — adding a few drops of hot sauce. Broil as usual. (Works on chicken as well.)

OR:
Here's a different kind of barbecue sauce you might like to try.

HONEY-MUSTARD SAUCE

1/2 stick margarine	1 T honey	1 t prepared mustard

Melt margarine and mix with honey and mustard. Brush on spare ribs or chicken before baking in a covered roaster pan in 350° oven. Cook until meat is tender. (Meat will brown as it cooks.)

BONUS HINT: If you simmer spare ribs for about 15 minutes before brushing with sauce and putting in oven, you'll extract a great deal of fat, and cut down on your roasting time.

BEANS, SOAKED

If you forgot to soak your beans overnight, and they're on today's menu — wash in a colander or strainer with hot water. Put in a pot and cover with water about 3 inches above the beans. Cover and boil for 5 minutes. Turn off heat and let set one to two hours, covered. Pour off this water and replace with fresh, then cook as usual.

BONUS HINT: Add one teaspoon ground ginger to the pot of beans when you start to cook them to prevent those gas attacks. There is no change of taste.

BEANS, VARIOUS

Did you know that you can substitute almost any variety of dry bean for another with pleasing results? (Lima beans are the exception.)

BEEF FOR STROGANOFF

No expensive beef cuts for this super dish? Try:

HAMBURGER STROGANOFF

1 medium onion, minced	2 T flour
1 lb. ground beef	2 t salt
1 clove garlic	1/4 t pepper
1/2 lb. mushrooms sliced	

1 can condensed cream of chicken soup, plus 1/2 soup can of water.
1 c commercial sour cream
Snipped parsley, chives or fresh dill

Saute first four ingredients 5 minutes. Sprinkle with flour, salt and pepper; add soup and water and simmer 10 minutes. Stir in sour cream. Garnish with parsley, chives or fresh dill, if desired.

Micro≈ Brown beef in non-metallic colander, place in 4-quart micro-wavable bowl. This takes 2 or 3 minutes for half the beef. Pour out fat, do rest of meat. Pour out all but a tablespoon of fat. Put onions and garlic in bowl and micro about 3 minutes. Add beef, sprinkle with flour, salt and pepper, add the can of soup, omitting the water. Micro 6 to 8 minutes, stirring once. Follow rest of directions.

OR:
Cooking liver in milk takes away the strong taste, and adding lemon juice gives a subtle flavor to the sauce similar to sour cream.

LIVER STROGANOFF

1 lb. liver, cut into	2 T oil or cooking spray
1/2 x 2 to 3-inch pieces	1 med. onion, chopped
1/2 c flour	1 clove garlic, minced
1 t salt	2 c milk (about)
1/2 t pepper	3 T lemon juice

Shake liver with flour, salt and pepper in plastic or brown bag to coat. Brown liver in oil, remove from pan; then saute onion until golden. Return liver to frying pan; add garlic, cover with milk, and simmer 25 to 30 minutes. Thicken sauce, if needed, with 1-2 T cornstarch mixed with a little water. Remove from heat. Stir in lemon juice. Serves 4 to 6.

BEEF, GROUND

MOCK MEATBALLS

1 1/2 c cracker crumbs	Pinch of ground sage
1 c (4 oz.) shredded	2 T fresh parsley, chopped
Cheddar cheese	4 eggs, beaten
1 c **finely** chopped walnuts	2 T oil
or pecans	Spaghetti sauce
1/4 t garlic powder	(or tomato sauce)
1/2 t salt	

Combine all ingredients except oil and sauce. Mix well and shape into one-inch balls. (Moisten your hands with water and balls won't stick to your hands while you're forming them.) Saute in oil, turning often to keep balls round. When brown, remove and drain well. Place in shallow casserole, pour sauce over, and bake at 350° for 45 minutes, or simmer in electric frying pan about 30 minutes. Serve over spaghetti and top with Parmesan cheese. Or simmer the balls in cream of mushroom soup and serve over noodles. Makes approximately 40 balls.

Micro≈ Follow regular directions, except shape into 36 one-inch balls. Place 12 at one time 1/2 inch apart in a circle around a 10-inch glass pie pan. Cover with wax paper and micro for 4 or 5 minutes. Freeze for later use, or put in micro-proof bowl, cover with tomato sauce or cream soup, micro for about 8 to 10 minutes, until hot. Pour over spaghetti, or noodles.

BERRIES, FOR JAM

FAKE BERRY JAM

4 c green tomatoes, cored and whirled in a blender
4 c sugar
2 small or 1 large package berry-flavored gelatin

In a large pan, bring green tomatoes and sugar to a rolling boil. Boil seven minutes. Remove from heat and stir in gelatin.
Put in sterilized jars and seal. Or pour into jelly glasses and cover with paraffin. Approximately 2 1/2 pints.

BONUS HINT: Heat sugar in oven while preparing fruit (or tomatoes in above recipe) — keeps jelly from scorching and the mixture comes to a rolling boil more quickly.

10

When you're out of ...

BREAD CRUMBS

A▶ Use finely crushed unsweetened breakfast cereal such as corn flakes, etc. Or try potato chips or instant potato flakes. Do NOT use wheat cereals, if allergic to wheat.

OR:
For a special flavor, put corn chips in a blender and whirl until fine to bread meat or fish.

BONUS HINT: The recipe calls for one cup of crumbs, and you're not sure how much of the uncrushed you'll need? Here's a "crumby count"

For one cup of crumbs you will need:
4 cups cornflakes
3 cups corn chips or potato chips
28 square soda crackers
4 slices of bread (a blender will turn even fresh bread into crumbs)

For pie crusts or other desserts, you'll need:
14 square graham crackers
22 vanilla wafers

OR:
If you need those missing bread crumbs for a meat loaf — try this differently delicious recipe which substitutes grated raw potato.

A▶   JOSIE'S MEAT LOAF

2 lb. ground beef	2 T catsup
1/2 lb. ground pork*	2 eggs
1 c grated raw potato	1 1/2 t salt
1 med. onion, chopped	1/4 t pepper
1 clove garlic, minced (optional)	

Mix together ingredients in order listed. Put into large greased bread pan. Bake at 350° for 1 1/2 hours. (Or bake in two smaller pans for about an hour.)
*You can use all beef.

Micro≈ Mix ingredients. Put into 10" pie plate. Micro for 15 to 20 minutes. Let set 10 minutes to firm. Cut in wedges to serve.

BONUS HINT: If you're out of fresh potatoes you can substitute frozen hash browns, or french fries. Put in about 3/4 cup.

When you're out of ...

BREAD CUBES (FOR STUFFING)

Dry out left-over bread in 150° oven, turning once. (Takes about an hour). Cut bread into cubes, and spread on cooking sheet. Air dry until all moisture is gone (a flat-top heating stove is ideal.) Store in tightly covered tin or jar.

BREAD STICKS

Make your own! Cut canned biscuits (ready to bake) in half. Roll each half in pencil-like stick. Brush with milk, roll in any dry crushed cereal plus 1 t. salt, or try sesame seed, celery, dill or caraway seeds. Bake in 450° oven 8 to 10 minutes until lightly brown. Air dry overnight.

OR:
You can also use your own biscuit recipe and proceed as above.

OR:
Yeast dough makes yummy sticks. When you're baking bread — make a small loaf (or loaves) instead of the large size, and use the extra dough for bread sticks. Follow the same recipe.

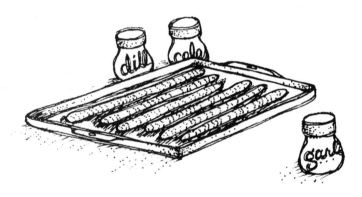

OR:
Slice day-old bread into strips. Dry out in slow oven until crisp and lightly browned.

OR:
If you've an abundance of bread heels, butter the bread side, slice into six strips and place on a cookie sheet, one layer deep, crust side down. Toast in a 300° oven. When the butter has melted in, turn and toast until dry and crisp. Sprinkle before or after toasting with celery salt, garlic salt, or a bit of grated cheese. Kids love them for after school snacks.

When you're out of ...

BUNS, FOR HAMBURGERS

This has to be planned for:

Keep a cut-in-half bread wrapper in freezer. Add pairs of bread heels until you have enough for your family. Hamburger time! Small youngsters with small appetites? Cut circle with 3-inch biscuit cutter from heels. (Save edges for bread crumbs.)

BUTTER

Just use margarine, no adjustments necessary.

OR:
Use shortening — but add 1/2 teaspoon salt per cup. This might make cookies a little crisper.

BUTTER, "REAL" OR TUB-TYPE SOFT MARGARINE

This is a super taste-alike for real butter, and stays soft even when cold. Do not use for frying, tends to scorch.

1 lb. margarine	1 c buttermilk	1/2 c salad oil

Unwrap the cubes of margarine while cold: place in a large bowl and let stand until extremely soft (but never melted).

Measure buttermilk into a two-cup measuring cup and then stir in the oil. With an electric mixer, beat the margarine until the cubes are blended. Add the buttermilk and oil mixture, about 1/4 cup at a time, beating until all liquid is absorbed. This will just about fill a two-pound plastic bowl.

BONUS HINT: This mixture freezes well (so does plain margarine, in case you want to stock up at a super sale), so I make four batches at a time — consecutively — to use up the one quart of buttermilk bought for this purpose.

When you're out of ...

BUTTER, SOFT

Butter or margarine too hard for easy spreading? Heat a small pan or heavy dish and invert over hard margarine or butter for a few minutes.

BUTTERMILK

Put 1 tablespoon vinegar or lemon juice in a measuring cup. Add enough fresh milk to make one cup. Let stand about 5 minutes.

OR:
If you're in a real hurry and have a microwave oven, place the above mixture in your microwave for 30 seconds. This saves on curdling time, which can vary from 5 to 15 minutes.

OR:
Replace buttermilk needed in cake or quick bread recipes with an equal amount of plain yogurt.

BONUS HINT: Buttermilk comes in dry form — and when reconstituted with water, gives the same results.

CAKE, FRESH

You have some pound cake, or other loaf cake which has been forgotten, and gotten a little dry — rejuvenate it into scrumptious:

MILLIE'S PUDDIN' CAKE

Take some old dry cake (pound cake, or an unfrosted loaf cake is best), some canned fruit, and leftover jelly — any kind. Use 1 cup of juice from the fruit plus 1/2 cup of sherry. Slice the cake, spread with jelly and cover the bottom of a bowl with about one-fourth of the slices. Drizzle with one-fourth of the fruit juice and one-fourth of the sherry. Top with a few pieces of fruit, then cover with a portion of soft custard (or vanilla pudding). Repeat layers and top it all with a whipped topping. Refrigerate until ready to serve.

When you're out of ...

CAKE MIX

Need a really special cake for a special birthday child?

A▶   POPCORN CAKE

> 17 c unsalted popcorn (be sure it's free of unpopped kernels)
> 3/4 c margarine or butter
> 1 large package (16 oz.) marshmallows
> Food coloring (optional)

Melt marshmallows and butter in top of double boiler. Add food coloring. While warm, pour over popcorn and mix gently until corn is well coated.

Press into a greased angel food pan. When cool, remove from pan; sprinkle decorator candies over top and sides. Slice with a serrated knife.

CAKE MIX, RIGHT FLAVOR

Need a chocolate cake and have only white or yellow cake mix? Add 2 to 3 tablespoons powdered baking cocoa.

If it's a lemon cake you want — replace 1/3 cup of the water called for in the recipe with 1/3 cup lemon juice. No other adjustments necessary in either case.

CAKE, OR OTHER BAKING PANS

8x1 1/2-inch round pan
Use: 10x6x2-inch dish; 9x1 1/2-inch round pan; 8x4x2-inch loaf pan; 9-inch pie plate. **Approximate volume: 1 1/2 quarts.**
8x8x2-inch pan
Use: 11x7 1/2x1 1/2-inch pan; 12x7 1/2x2-inch pan, 9x5x3-inch loaf pan; TWO 8x1 1/2-inch round pans. **Approximate volume:** *2 quarts.*
13x9x2-inch pan
Use: 14x11x2-inch baking dish: TWO 9x1 1/2-inch round pans; THREE 8x1 1/2-inch round pans. **Approximate volume:** 3 quarts.

CAKE PANS

Bake cake mix, or your own "scratch" cake in greased and floured cans. Creamed soup, or vegetable cans are the right size. Fill half full, and bake according to directions for layer cakes. When cool, cut in 1/4-inch slices and put frosting between two slices. Not so messy for lunches as layer cakes, and less calories per serving.

*ℯ some candy, but don't want it too rich, and can't
and beat, try one of these quickies.*

SS►   ORANGE SWEET TREATS

1/2 c (1 stick) butter or
   margarine
1/2 c firmly packed brown
   sugar or brown sugar
   substitute
1/2 c orange juice

1 t grated orange rind
2 c quick-cooking rolled oats
1/2 c chopped walnuts
Flaked coconut
   or finely crushed cookie
   crumbs

Melt butter in medium saucepan; add brown sugar, orange rind and orange juice, stirring until sugar is dissolved. Remove from heat.

Stir in rolled oats and nuts. Spread into an 8x8x2 inch pan. Freeze, then cut into 2x1 inch bars, or refrigerate 1 hour, then shape into balls and roll in coconut.

Micro≈ Mix first four ingredients in a 4-cup glass measuring cup; micro for 4 minutes, until butter is melted and sugar dissolved. Stir once or twice. Pour over oats and walnuts. Mix well. Now follow regular directions.

OR:
SS►   PINEAPPLE CANDY

1 c crushed pineapple
   (packed in its own juice),
   drained
3/4 c coconut
1 t vanilla

3/4 t butter flavoring
   (optional)
2 T sugar or sugar substitute
2 cups non fat dry milk

Combine pineapple, flavorings and sugar in a mixer on low speed. Gradually add nonfat dry milk until consistency of frosting. Add more dry milk if necessary. Drop by spoonfuls on cookie sheet and freeze for 1/2 hour.

OR:
Children love making these, especially when they hide a raisin, small piece of walnut meat or miniature marshmallow in the middle of each ball for a tasty surprise.

HONEY-CRUNCHIES

1 c chunky peanut butter	1/2 c nonfat dry milk powder
3/4 c honey	20 graham cracker squares
1 c shredded coconut or toasted wheat germ.	

Combine peanut butter, honey and milk in large mixing bowl. Crush graham crackers into fine crumbs, and add to peanut butter mixture. Mix with hands until well blended. Roll into balls — a tablespoon at a time, then roll each ball in coconut or wheat germ.

When you're out of ...

CELERY, FOR FLAVOR

Another plan-ahead, for the time you may be out ...

FLAVOR CUBES

Put left-over celery leaves, coarse or limp stalks, etc. into blender with chopped onion and enough water to whirl. Blend at high speed until thoroughly minced. Put mixture into ice-cube trays and freeze solid. Remove from tray and store in plastic freezer bags.

Now you have celery and onion flavoring whenever you need it, and if you have kids that object to onion or celery chunks — they'll never know! Extra zucchini, or other vegetable bits can be tossed into the blender, too. You can even "blenderize" left-over tossed salad — if the vinegar comes on a bit too strong, add a dash of sugar. Good healthy flavoring for soups, stews, spaghetti sauce.

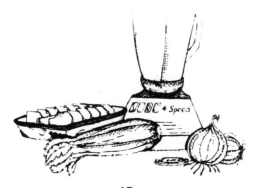

17

When you're out of ...

CHEESECLOTH, FOR SPICE OR GARNI BAG

If you need just a small amount of spices — as in pickle-making — you can carefully remove the staple from a tea bag, pour out the tea and put in your pickling spices; stabling the bag shut again.

Need a larger bag? Use a cup-shaped coffee filter — just fill and tie.

OR:

Put flavoring ingredients into a metal tea ball, hang on the edge of the pot, and let the flavor seep through. This is a good technique if the children or grandchildren object to seeing onion or garlic in the sauce or stew. With the objectionable chunks in the tea-steeper, you can remove the evidence after extracting the flavor.

CHOCOLATE CHIPS FOR MELTING

Why spend money on expensive chips only to melt them? You can use these substitutions for 12 ounces of semi-sweet chips.

CHOCOLATE CHIP EXCHANGE

1 1/2 c cocoa	1/2 c oil	1/2 c sugar

Stir together in a 2 cup glass measuring cup and heat for a minute or two in the microwave. Or put in a small pan over medium heat and stir until the chocolate is melted and the sugar dissolved.

OR:

You can melt 8 ounces (1 ounce each) of baking chocolate and stir in 1/2 cup of sugar.

When you're out of ...

CHOCOLATE OR COCOA

When you need a chocolate frosting and have neither of the above —try melting a chocolate candy bar, mixed with about one cup of powdered sugar and a teaspoon of vanilla, with enough milk (added very sparingly) to a spreading or drizzling consistency.

No candy bar? Try three tablespoons of hot chocolate drink mix and follow the same directions. (Notice that no butter or margarine is used — cuts down on calories and fat.)

SS▶   CHOCOLATE (OR COCOA) DRINK MIX

Make your own — quick and easy!

> 1 1/2 c nonfat dry milk powder
> 1/2 c sugar or sugar substitute
> 6 T cocoa

Mix together, then put 2 rounded tablespoons in each glass or cup. Add water, hot or cold. Makes 6 to 8 cups.

OR:
If you want to make a bit richer mixture in a larger quantity, try this keep-on-hand recipe.

HOT COCOA MIX

> 1 8 qt. box (10 cups) nonfat dry milk
> 1 6 oz. jar powdered coffee creamer
> 1 lb. powdered sugar
> 1 8 oz. box baking cocoa

Mix together and store in tightly covered container. Makes four quarts of mix. Use 3 heaping tablespoons per cup of hot water.

If you have calorie-counters or diabetics in the family, use sugar substitutes in the above recipes, and you'll have a treat they can enjoy.

When you're out of ...

CHOCOLATE SAUCE

COCOA SYRUP

1/3 c cocoa	1 c water
1 c sugar	1 t vanilla
1/4 t salt	2 T cornstarch

Mix all ingredients except vanilla in a saucepan and boil 3 minutes, stirring until smooth. Let cool and add vanilla. Store in refrigerator in covered jar. Use as sauce over ice cream or cake. May also be used for hot or cold cocoa drinks — just add 2 tablespoons for each cup of milk.

OR:

CHOCO-FUDGE SAUCE

2 T shortening, melted	3/4 c granulated sugar
6 T cocoa	1/2 t vanilla
1 c nonfat dry milk	1/2 t salt
1/2 c warm water	1/3 c hot water

Combine shortening and cocoa in top of double boiler. In a small bowl, thoroughly mix dry milk and *warm* water. Add to cocoa mixture, then stir in sugar, vanilla and salt. Place over boiling water and cook —stirring until sugar is dissolved and mixture begins to thicken. Stir in the hot water. Let cool, then pour into a container with a lid. Cover and refrigerate. If sauce gets too thick, thin by adding hot water, 1 tablespoon at a time.

CHOCOLATE SQUARES, SEMI-SWEET

Use 1 T shortening or oil and 3 T unsweetened cocoa for each square of chocolate, plus 3 teaspoons of sugar.

CHOCOLATE SQUARES, UNSWEETENED

Omit the sugar in the above recipe.
If you need to start with melted chocolate, melt the butter in a tiny saucepan, then stir in cocoa.

CINNAMON

For apple or peach pie, add a small handful of "red hots" just before putting on top crust. Delicious, and adds a pretty pink color.

When you're out of ...

COCONUT

Here's a fun cake to try — and if you have a smidgen of coconut to sprinkle on the frosting, (or even if you don't) you'll have everyone guessing when you bake:

CHOCOLATE SAUERKRAUT CAKE

2 1/4 c sifted flour	2/3 c shortening
1 t baking powder	1 1/2 c sugar
1/2 t salt	1 1/2 t vanilla
1 t soda	3 eggs
1/2 c cocoa	1 c water

2/3 c rinsed, drained, chopped sauerkraut

Sift together dry ingredients. Cream shortening and sugar, then add vanilla and eggs — mixing well. Add dry ingredients, alternately with water. Add sauerkraut and mix thoroughly. Pour into well-greased 9x13-inch pan. Bake at 375° for 35 minutes. Can be baked in two 8-inch round cake pans for about 25 minutes.

COOKIES

Need some cookies in a hurry? Spread graham crackers with canned or homemade (even leftover) frosting. Cap with a second cracker.

OR:
No frosting? Try mixing 1/2 cup powdered sugar with enough milk for a thick, paste-like consistency. Spread between two graham crackers.

OR:
Heat 1/2 cup honey. Stir in dry milk powder until spreadable.

Micro≈ Heat the honey in a 2-cup glass measure for 1 to 1 1/2 minutes. Then add dry milk powder.

OR:
GRAHAM CRACKER FREEZE

Spread instant pudding (any flavor) about 1/2 inch thick on graham crackers. (Mix up the pudding first.) Top with another cracker, pressing lightly. Put in freezer, uncovered, for about 1 hour. When firm, wrap individually in foil or plastic and package in freezer containers.
Eat frozen, otherwise filling squishes out.

A▶ CORNMEAL

Just substitute any kind of uncooked cereal (such as Malt-O-Meal, Cream of Wheat, Wheat-hearts, etc.) The flavors in quick breads or other recipes are not identical, but the texture is similar and the results are pleasing. These cereals can also be used for "breading" fish or for "flouring" bread pans.

CORN SYRUP

Boil together 1/2 cup water and 1/2 cup sugar for three minutes. Cool and use as directed in recipe.

OR:
Use 1 cup sugar plus 1/4 cup water for each cup of corn syrup.

COTTAGE CHEESE

Lasagna sounds good for the dinner menu and, when you reach for the cottage cheese, you find that somebody polished off all but a small dab? Use white sauce instead; you'll be pleasantly surprised.

CREAMY LASAGNA

1/2 lb. lasagna noodles

TOMATO-MEAT FILLING

1/2 lb. ground beef	1 can (12 oz.) tomato sauce
1 med. onion, chopped	1/4 t garlic salt
1 sm. green pepper, chopped	1/2 t each basil, oregano
	Sugar
Salt & Pepper to taste	1/2 c grated Parmesan cheese

Brown beef, stir in onions. Cook briefly. Add rest of Tomato-Meat Filling, except cheese. Simmer 15 min.

WHITE SAUCE*

1/3 c margarine	1/4 t pepper	1/3 c flour
1/8 t onion powder	1/2 t salt	2 c warm milk

1/2 pkg. (10 oz.) frozen, chopped spinach, drained (optional, but good!)

Micro≈ (White Sauce only) Place margarine, flour and seasonings in a 4-cup measure. Micro about 1 minute, until butter is melted. Stir in milk and cook 3 to 4 minutes. Stir every minute until bubbling and thick. (Note: milk may be cold — but may take longer.)

Melt margarine. Stir in seasonings and flour to make a paste. Slowly add milk, stirring constantly over medium heat until thickened.

Now put it all together.

Cook lasagna noodles until fork-tender. Rinse with cold water. Grease an 8x11-inch baking pan. Pour 1/4 of the white sauce into pan; spread evenly. Lay lasagna noodles (one-noodle deep) over sauce. Cover with 1/3 meat sauce. Sprinkle lightly with Parmesan cheese.

Repeat this layering twice more, ending with a layer of lasagna noodles. Spread with white sauce and sprinkling of Parmesan cheese. Cover and bake at 375° for 45 minutes. Let rest 10 or 15 minutes out of the oven before serving.

If desired, 5 minutes before the end of baking time, uncover. Place slices of melting cheese (or sprinkle grated American, Cheddar or Jack on top). Return to oven. Ready when cheese is melted. Serves 6 to 8.

When you're out of ...

CREAM

When a recipe calls for a small amount of cream, substitute a dab of vanilla ice cream.

OR:

Use nondairy creamer — mixing one part powder to same amount of very hot water.

NOTE: **One** cup of powdered creamer dissolved in **one** cup of hot water yields one cup "cream". (A case where one plus one does not equal two!)

OR:
A▶

Add the richness of cream, without the cost, to any cream soup you're making from scratch by adding some non-dairy creamer.

OR:

CREAM, LIGHT

1 cup of undiluted evaporated milk can be substituted for 1 cup of light cream. Or plop 2 tablespoons of butter or margarine in a measuring cup and add milk to the 1 cup line. (If the butter and milk have to be kept separate, just reduce each cup of milk by 2 tablespoons and add 2 tablespoons of butter.)

When you're out of ...

LF▶ CREAM SOUP

*One of the most time- and money-saving recipes came from Iowa.
This handy mix can be used any time canned cream soup is required.*

LF▶   GWEN'S CREAM SOUP MIX

2 c instant non-fat dry milk   1/2 t pepper
3/4 c cornstarch   1 t basil, optional
1/4 c instant chicken   1 t thyme, optional
   bouillon*
2 T dried onion flakes

Combine all ingredients. Mix well. Store in glass jar with tight lid.
This mix makes three cups — equal to 9 cans (10 1/2 oz.) cream soup.
To make the equivalent of one can of soup, combine 1/3 cup of mix with
1 1/4 cups of water. (Easy method — stir into 1/4 cup cold water; add to
1 cup boiling water in pan and stir over low heat until thick.) If desired,
add 1 tablespoon butter, chopped mushrooms, cooked celery or dried
herbs.

*You have only bouillon cubes? They crush easily with a rolling pin.
One cube equals one tablespoon.

For cream of tomato soup, replace the water with tomato juice.

CROUTONS

Use the bread cubes you made or get the packaged variety. Drizzle a
little salad oil, melted butter or margarine over the cubes spread on a
cookie sheet. Toast in 300° oven a few minutes. You can sprinkle on
garlic salt, or onion salt for extra flavor.

CUCUMBER

Try raw tender, young zucchini, sliced thin to add crispness to that
tossed salad ... or fresh cauliflower ... or jicama ... or water chestnuts.

When you're out of ...

DOUGHNUTS

Use canned biscuits (any variety). Put thumbs in the middle of each biscuit to make a hole. Stretch a little and turn inside out to make a ring. Fry in 1/4 inch fat in frying pan. Sprinkle with cinnamon sugar.

OR:
Try this time-saver, using frozen bread dough for light and airy

EASY DOUGHNUTS

1 loaf frozen bread dough, thawed one hour
Oil for frying   Cinnamon sugar   Powdered sugar

Slice the partially frozen dough into 1/4-inch thick circles. With thumbs, gently push a hole in the middle of the circles, and turn inside out. (This dough is harder to handle than the canned biscuits, and the rings are a bit lop-sided, but after the frying they become more rounded.) Place circles on a cookie sheet, cover and let rise 1/2 hour. Fry in oil, or melted shortening, about 1/4 inch deep. Turn once. Drain on paper towels, then roll in cinnamon sugar or powdered sugar.

Our contributor suggests pinching off dough into one-inch balls before placing on baking sheets to rise, to make DOUGHNUT BALLS. These were easier, but not quite as light as the rings.

DOUGHNUT CUTTER

Who says doughnuts have to be round? Cut dough in squares with a knife; then punch out the hole. (Can use an apple corer.) Saves time and no scraps to re-roll.

25

When you're out of ...

DRESSING FOR SALAD

Here's a dressing that is excellent for potato salad or any vegetable combination. Nice on sliced tomatoes or in a tossed green salad. Also good served as a dip with the addition of chopped green onion and celery with a shred or two of grated carrot for color.

CREAMY BUTTERMILK SALAD DRESSING

1 c buttermilk	1 t garlic powder
1 c mayonnaise	1/8 t pepper
1/2 t salt	1/2 t oregano
2 t parsley flakes	1/2 t basil

Mix in 1 quart jar. Keep covered in refrigerator. Keeps for one week or more.

OR:

Here's an interesting dressing, with canned soup for its base.

TOMATO SOUP DRESSING

1 can (10 3/4 oz.) can condensed tomato soup

1/3 c vinegar	dash of red pepper
1/2 c salad oil	pinch of paprika
1 t prepared mustard	1/4 c sugar
1 t grated onion	1 t salt

Put in jar and shake well. Store in refrigerator.

OR:

For a low-calorie toss for salads, try:

LC▶   COTTAGE CHEESE SALAD DRESSING

1/2 c cottage cheese	1 t lemon juice
3 T celery, chopped	or vinegar
2 T onion, chopped	1/2 t garlic salt
Dash of pepper	

Whirl all ingredients in blender until smooth. Chill well.

When you're out of ...

EASTER EGG DYES

Use food coloring if Easter egg dyes are unavailable. Let children experiment with the charts on food-coloring box. Make "resist" designs on the eggs with color crayons.

OR:
Paint **blown** egg shells with nail polish. (Never use on eggs to be eaten — may be toxic.) Gives eggs a glossy, enamelled look. Two coats create a mottled effect.

EGGS

One of the most intriguing substitutions for eggs came from a cookbook printed in 1815. The language is so quaint, I must share it with you:

A▶
"Snow is an excellent substitute for eggs, either in puddings or pancakes. Two large spoonfuls will supply the place of one egg ... This is a useful piece of information, especially as snow falls at the season when eggs are dearest.

"The snow may be taken up from any clean spot before it is wanted, and will not lose its virtue; though the sooner it is used the better."

SNOW PANCAKES are truly delicious.

OR:
If it's summer time and no snow is available, you can cook muffins or pancakes without eggs — compensate with a little extra water.

27

EGGS (cont.)

You're all set to bake a cake, some cookies or a quick bread and not one egg?

A▶

Substitute 1 t cornstarch for each omitted egg adding 3 T water for each t cornstarch.

This was tried on several different brands of cake mix including one which called for 3 eggs. There was a slight change of texture, depending on the brand used. (One was slightly dry and crumbly, and another was super moist and tender.) When you need to substitute only one egg, there is no discernible change.
Naturally, this will not work with chiffon, sponge or angel food cake when the whipped volume of the eggs is essential.

OR:

If you are one egg short, reach for the mayonnaise jar and use a scant 1/4 cup mayonnaise for the missing egg. Follow package directions and the cake will be delicious.

OR:

Instead of a beaten egg to dip foods before rolling in flour or crumbs, use mayonnaise or salad dressing. Apply to each piece with a pastry brush.

OR:

Here's a lovely cool dessert that uses no eggs ... and no one will ever believe you! Vary the flavor (and color) of gelatin to suit the season.

A▶   MILE-HIGH PIE

1 pkg. (3 oz.) gelatin, any flavor	1/2 c chilled grapefruit juice or lemon juice
6 T sugar	2 T lemon juice - used later
1/2 c nonfat dry milk	

1 8-inch baked pie shell

Dissolve gelatin and sugar in 1 cup boiling water. Stir in 1/2 cup cold water. Chill. Combine dry milk and grapefruit or lemon juice. Beat until soft peaks form. Add the 2 T extra lemon juice and beat until stiff. Mix in slightly jelled gelatin mixture. Chill 20 minutes. Pour into pie shell. Chill several hours. Serves six.

OR:

Here are some "scratch cakes" to try, with no eggs involved.

A▶ ## NO-EGG RAISIN CAKE

2 c water	1 c chopped nuts (if desired)
1 c raisins	1 3/4 c flour
1/2 c butter or margarine	1 c sugar
1/2 t each cinnamon, salt	1 t baking soda
and nutmeg	
Ice cream or whipped topping (optional)	

Bring water and raisins to boil in saucepan, and simmer 10 minutes. Add butter and let cool while you mix dry ingredients. Blend well into raisins and water. Stir in nuts. Pour into greased 9-inch square pan and bake in preheated 350° oven 40 minutes. Test with toothpick in center.

A▶ ## EGGLESS APPLESAUCE CAKE

2 c flour	2 t baking soda
1 t each nutmeg and cinnamon	1 c nutmeats
3 T cocoa	1 c raisins
1 t cornstarch	1 1/2 c applesauce
1 c sugar	1/2 c salad oil

Sift dry ingredients, add raisins and nuts, then applesauce and oil. Beat well. Bake in greased 9x13 pan in 325° oven. Good without nuts, with a few extra raisins, or try a cup of Toasted Oatmeal.

When you're out of ...

EGGS AND MILK

Don't let the name "Biscuits" fool you. These rich and crunchy cookies are of Australian origin which may explain the name.

A▶ ## ANZAC BISCUITS

1 c rolled oats	1/2 c butter
1 c coconut	1 T dark corn syrup
1 c flour	1 t soda
1 c sugar	2 T boiling water

Combine dry ingredients in a bowl, and make a well in the center. Melt butter and syrup. Add soda mixed with boiling water, then pour this mixture into dry ingredients.

Mix to a moist but firm consistency. Drop by tablespoonfuls onto cold greased cookie sheet. Bake at 250° about 20 minutes.

OR

Try a cake with a "mystery ingredient" — a favorite of the recipe-giver at Christmas time.

A▶   CHRISTMAS CAKE

3/4 c butter or shortening	1 t ground cloves
1 1/2 c sugar	1 1/2 t each nutmeg, cinnamon
3 c sifted flour	1 c cream of tomato soup
1/4 t salt	3/4 c water
3 t baking powder	1 1/2 c chopped nuts
1 t baking soda	1 1/2 c raisins

Cream butter or shortening and add sugar slowly.

Sift dry ingredients and add to creamed mixture, alternately with the tomato soup combined with the water. Mix thoroughly. Add the raisins and nuts and pour into a well-greased tube pan with removable bottom. Bake for 1 hour at 350°.

Need a new frosting idea for this cake?

MARGARET'S CREAM CHEESE FROSTING

2 pkg. (3 oz.) cream cheese	3 c powdered sugar
1 egg yolk	1/8 t salt
	1 t vanilla

Work cream cheese with fork until soft and creamy. Add egg yolk and mix well. Add sugar (about a cup at a time), mixing thoroughly after each addition. Stir in salt and vanilla.

OR:

Try these fruit filled gems.

A▶   PINEAPPLE WHOLE-WHEAT MUFFINS

1 c white flour	1 t salt
1 c whole wheat flour	1 sm. can crushed pineapple
1/4 c packed brown sugar	1/4 c oil
3 t baking powder	

Mix flours, sugar and baking powder together. Pour undrained pineapple into a large measuring cup. Add water to bring fruit and juice to 2 cups. Stir into flour mixture — combining quickly. Add oil. Pour into greased muffin tins. NOTE: Muffin tins may be filled nearly to the top. These muffins are moist and light, but they do not rise much. Bake in 350° oven for 20 minutes or a bit longer. Makes 12 muffins.

When you're out of ...

EGGS AND SHORTENING

When you've promised the family some muffins, and find the cupboard almost bare — try these.

EMERGENCY MUFFINS

2 c self-rising flour	2 t sugar
1 c milk	5 T mayonnaise

Mix all ingredients together, stirring until just blended. Pour into greased muffin tins. Bake at 400° for 10-15 minutes. Makes 12 muffins.

No self-rising flour? Add 3 teaspoons baking powder and 1/2 teaspoon salt to all-purpose flour.

OR:

Even with no eggs or shortening, you can make

A▶   RAISIN BRAN BREAD

Sift together:	Stir in:
1 1/2 c flour	1/2 c raisins
1/2 c white or brown sugar	1/2 c chopped nuts
1 t baking soda	1 c All-Bran cereal
1/2 t salt	Add: 1 c buttermilk. Stir.

Pour into greased and floured 4x8-inch loaf pan. Bake at 300° for 1 hour or until done.

EGGS, MILK AND SHORTENING

Surprise yourself and your family, too, when you serve this excellent spice cake; with mayonnaise providing the eggs and shortening.

A▶   SPICY MAYONNAISE CAKE

Mix together:	Add to dry ingredients:
2 c flour	1 c mayonnaise **or**
2 t soda	1 c salad dressing
1 t cinnamon	(the kind that comes in a jar)
1/4 t ground cloves	1 c water
1/4 t nutmeg	1/2 c raisins
1 c sugar	1/2 c chopped nuts
1/8 t salt	

Mix thoroughly and pour batter into greased and floured 9x13-inch cake pan. Bake at 350° for 30 minutes.

31

OR:

Out of eggs and shortening? The title tells the "in lieu" ingredient.

MAYONNAISE CAKE

1 c dates (or raisins), chopped	1 t soda
1 c hot water	1 c chopped nuts

Stir together and let set while you mix:
1 c sugar, 3 T cocoa, 1 c mayonnaise
Mix thoroughly and add to fruit and nut mixture. Then stir in:
1 2/3 c flour, 1 t vanilla
Bake in 350° oven 40 minutes in oblong pan.

OR:

Here's an even easier version and you can use salad dressing.

SALAD DRESSING CAKE

Sift together: 2 c flour, 1 c sugar, 1/2 c cocoa, 1/2 t salt, 2 t soda. Blend in: 1 c salad dressing or mayonnaise and 1 c cold water. Bake 30 minutes at 350° in 9x13 pan.

When you're out of ...

EGGS, ENOUGH

If you need to stretch scrambled eggs, add 2 tablespoons cottage cheese to replace one egg. Keep the ratio at 2 eggs used to one egg omitted.

Or add tofu in the same proportions.

EGG POACHER

Remove both ends from a tuna fish can, clean thoroughly. When it's time to poach eggs, put the can in simmering water, drop the eggs into it, and you'll have a nicely shaped poached egg.

EGGS, WHOLE

If you've whipped up all your egg whites, and you're ready for a recipe that calls for whole eggs, you can substitute two of those leftover egg yolks for each whole egg called for.

When you're out of ...

EVERYTHING, ALMOST

It has been one of those days, and it seems there's nothing in the house; but you do have bread, catsup and cheese. The kids will even pass on "the recipe" to their friends.

LAST-MINUTE PIZZAS

Bread (any kind — white, whole wheat, French, English muffins ...)
Catsup, garlic powder or salt, and oregano
Cheese — whatever's handy

Spread bread with catsup; sprinkle with seasonings. Break up (or coarsely grate) cheese over all. Broil until cheese melts.

OR:
For a more adult-type breakfast, lunch or supper try:

ARMENIAN STYLE OMELET

Eggs (as many as you need) slightly beaten (1 or 2 per person)
About one green onion per egg, chopped — tops are best
Shortening or oil

Mix eggs and onions together. Melt shortening in frying pan   (or heat oil) just enough to coat the bottom. Pour in egg and onion mixture. When the omelet bottom is brown, loosen around the edges. Place a flat lid or plate on top of pan. Quickly invert omelet, then slide it back into frying pan to brown other side. Cut in wedges and serve.

OR:
Only a couple of cans in the cupboard? Here's a quickie:

BACK-AGAINST-THE-WALL SUPPER

1 can cream of mushroom or celery soup
1 can (6 1/2 oz.) tuna, drained

Prepare soup, using 1/2 can of water. Heat to piping hot. Add tuna and stir to mingle flavors. Serve over rice, noodles, toast — whatever's left in the cupboard!
(And if you're out of cream soup, look on page 24.)

When you're out of ...

FAT REMOVER

No syringe for pulling off the fat from stew or soup? The best way to get rid of the most fat is to pour the liquid into a bowl and set in refrigerator overnight until the fat rises to the top and hardens. If you have to serve the dish right away, sop up the fat with paper towels or even facial tissues; or float the outer leaf of a head of lettuce on top and swish gently until fat is absorbed.

FLOUR

When you're making a cake from a mix, and you have no flour for dusting your cake pan — save a bit of the cake mix to use instead.

OR:
Use wheat germ. This is a good idea even if you have flour — the wheat germ adds nourishment and flavor. Especially good with breads — quick or yeast.

OR:
A▶ Make your own oatmeal flour by whirling quick cooking oats in your blender. Use 1 1/3 cups oatmeal flour to 1 cup whole wheat. But if you're substituting for white flour, make it 3/4 cup oat flour for each cup of white. Oat flour is especially good for pancakes — reminiscent of buckwheat.

OR:
If you have only self-rising flour — eliminate the baking powder and salt in the recipe.

OR:
Need to make some cookies? An infinite variety can be made from this basic recipe.

CAKE MIX COOKIES

1 box cake mix — any kind
1/4 c oil
2 eggs

Mix half the cake mix with oil and eggs. Then add rest of mix. You can add a 6 ounce bag of chocolate chips to a yellow cake; a cup of nuts or cup of coconut (or a combination) to any flavor cake mix.
Drop by teaspoon onto ungreased baking sheet. Bake in 375° oven for about 12 minutes.

FLOUR AND MILK

For those of you allergic to wheat and/or milk, here are three cookie recipes to satisfy your sweet tooth.

A▶   LACY OATMEAL COOKIES

2 c quick-cooking oatmeal	2 T shortening
3 t baking powder	(at room temperature)
1/2 t salt	2 eggs
1 c brown sugar	1/2 c raisins

Mix together dry ingredients. Add shortening and eggs. Beat until well-blended; then fold in raisins. Drop from teaspoon onto greased baking sheet, 2 inches apart. Bake at 350° for 10 to 12 minutes.

Remove from baking sheet immediately.

A▶   RAISIN OATMEAL COOKIES

2 T melted shortening	1/2 t almond extract
1 c sugar	1/2 t baking powder
2 eggs	3/4 t salt
1/2 t vanilla	2 c rolled oats

Combine melted shortening and sugar. Add eggs and beat until light and fluffy. Add flavorings. Mix together baking powder, salt and oats and add to first mixture.

Drop from teaspoon onto greased baking sheet, 2 inches apart. Bake at 350° for 12 to 15 minutes. Remove from baking sheets immediately.

OR:

Let puffed rice help you fill the cookie jar.

A▶   PEANUT BUTTER SQUARES

5 c puffed rice	1/3 c peanut butter
1/4 c margarine	1/2 lb. marshmallows
	(32 large)

Crisp puffed rice in 350° oven for 10 minutes. Place in large bowl. Melt margarine, peanut butter and marshmallows in double boiler. Pour over puffed rice, stirring well.

Pack into shallow greased pan; cool and cut in squares.

OR:

You'll never believe how light and fluffy these cookies turn out, with so few ingredients.

A▶   PEANUT BUTTER COOKIES

1 c peanut butter	1 egg
1 c sugar (white or brown)	1 t vanilla (optional)

Mix all ingredients together. (Do not use electric beater.) Drop by teaspoon onto ungreased baking sheet. Press with a fork dipped in water, if desired. Bake in 325° oven for 12 to 13 minutes. No longer!

When you're out of ...

FLOUR, ANY KIND

Let cold breakfast cereal help you fill the cookie jar.

A▶   COCONUT CRUNCH COOKIES

2 egg whites	2 c corn flakes
1 c brown sugar	1/2 c chopped nuts
1 c coconut	1/2 t vanilla

Beat egg whites stiff. Add brown sugar and beat well. Stir in remaining ingredients. Drop from teaspoon on well-greased cookie sheet. Bake 15 to 20 minutes in 325° oven.

OR:

A▶   CRISPIE TREATS

1/4 c butter or margarine
10 oz. pkg. regular marshmallows (about 40) or
    4 c miniature marshmallows
5 c crispy-rice ready-to-eat cereal

Add marshmallows to melted margarine (in a large saucepan). Stir constantly until marshmallows melt and the mixture is syrupy. Remove from heat.

Add cereal and stir until well coated with marshmallow mixture. Use a buttered spatula to press mixture firmly into buttered 13x9x2 inch pan. Cut into 1x2 oblongs when cool.

Micro≈ Melt butter in 3 quart casserole (takes about 1 minute). Add marshmallows and microwave 2 1/2 to 3 minutes. Remove from oven and stir until thoroughly mixed. Follow regular directions.

OR:
This time quick cooking rolled oats take the place of flour.

A▶ **BOILED COOKIES**

Have measured, so you can add quickly to the boiled ingredients.

3 c quick-cooking oats	1 t vanilla
1/2 c peanut butter	Dash of salt
1/2 to 1 c nuts or coconut	

Then mix together in a saucepan:

2 c sugar	1/2 c margarine
3 T cocoa	1/2 c milk

Bring to a boil and boil for one minute. Remove from heat and add premeasured ingredients. Drop from teaspoon onto wax paper covered cookie sheets. Let cool completely before removing. Makes about 50 cookies.

Micro≈ Put first five ingredients into a large bowl. Mix sugar, cocoa, margarine and milk in a 3 or 4 cup glass measure. Micro for about 3 minutes, stirring every minute, until just beginning to bubble. Then pour over oat mixture in bowl. When mixed follow regular directions.

OR:
If you're in a cake-baking mood, have run out of mixes, and the flour canister is bare — try:

GRAHAM NUT CAKE

1/4 c butter or margarine	1/2 t cloves if desired
3/4 c sugar	2 t baking powder
1 egg	1 c finely chopped walnuts
1 t cinnamon	1 c milk
2 c finely rolled graham crackers (25 squares)	

Cream butter and sugar until light and fluffy. Add egg and beat well. Combine cracker crumbs, spices and nuts. Add to creamed mixture, then the milk and beat well.

Bake in a well-greased 8x8x2 pan in 350° oven. Cut in squares and serve warm with whipped topping. Or dust with powdered sugar and serve cold.

If the batter is baked in a 9x13 pan, you can cut it into bars (after it has cooled) for a cake-like cookie. Good for lunch boxes.

OR:

A torte-like cake, this richer version using graham crackers, makes a show-off dessert for company.

GRAHAM CREAM CAKE

1/2 c butter	1/4 t salt
1 c sugar	2 1/2 t baking powder
3 eggs, separated	1 c chopped pecans or
2/3 c milk	walnuts
2 c graham crackers,	1 t vanilla
crushed fine (25 squares)	2 c whipping cream

Cream butter and sugar until fluffy. Add beaten egg yolks, milk, salt and beat well. Mix cracker crumbs with baking powder and 1/2 cup chopped nuts. Blend with first mixture. Add vanilla and fold in stiffly beaten egg whites. Bake in two greased 8″ cake pans in 375° oven about 25 minutes. Cool. Spread cream (whipped with 2 tablespoons sugar and 1 teaspoon vanilla) between layers and on top. Sprinkle with remaining nuts.

When you're out of ...

FLOUR, CAKE

Reduce regular flour by 2 tablespoons per cup after sifting, or keep the full cup and add 1 tablespoon cornstarch.

When you're out of ...

FLOUR, ENOUGH

If you lack about half a cup of flour in any baked goods, just substitute oatmeal, unground. Use a little less amount than the flour you're replacing. Gives a nut-like flavor.

OR:
If you're short about half the flour needed for making muffins or quick breads, you can use crushed unsweetened cold cereal or quick or old-fashioned rolled oats. (If you don't like the texture the oats will give, put them in your blender for a quick oat "flour").

OR:
For small "shortages", you can use biscuit mix for flour you are lacking. Just mix with the flour you do have.

OR:
In the middle of making a pie crust and you're a bit short of flour? Make up the difference with pancake and waffle flour — up to 1/3 of the total.

FLOUR, MILK AND EGGS

Whether you're allergic to, or just don't have any of the above — you can still enjoy these cookies. Whirling the oatmeal into flour gives the cookies a smooth texture.

A▶   GINGER COOKIES

1/2 c light molasses	1 t ginger
1/4 c margarine	1/2 t salt
2 1/2 c rolled oats	1/4 t baking soda
1/4 c sugar	

Heat molasses to boiling point, pour over margarine. Put oats into blender and grind into flour. Measure 2 cups.

Mix together dry ingredients until well-blended. Add molasses mixture and mix well. Drop from teaspoon on ungreased cookie sheets and bake at 375° for 10 to 12 minutes.

FLOUR, REGULAR

If you have only cake flour, add 2 tablespoons per cup.

When you're out of ...

FLOUR, SELF-RISING

For each cup, put 2 teaspoons baking powder, and 1/2 teaspoon salt in a cup. Fill with regular flour and mix well.

FLOUR, TO THICKEN GRAVY

Use 1 tablespoon cornstarch for each tablespoon flour. This will reduce the cooking time and the calories.

Add dry bread crumbs or cracker crumbs till gravy thickens. You can even pull a slice of fresh bread into pieces and stir until thickened.

If you're out of all of the above, try instant potato flakes.

FOOD COLORING

In a quandary because you've promised a pink frosting for your youngster's birthday cake and the food-coloring bottle is dry? Add 1/2 cup red pre-sweetened soft-drink mix (dry) to your white butter-cream frosting. Unsweetened drink mix may also be used — just add a teaspoon at a time until you get the color desired. If you make a cherry cake, and use cherry-flavored mix — your frosting will be taste- **and** color coordinated. Think of the unlimited taste and color combinations!

FREEZER CONTAINERS

In addition to cottage cheese cartons, those large thin plastic milk shake or soft drink "glasses" with plastic lids from fast food restaurants make excellent freezer containers. If there's a hole in the lid where the straw goes through, cover the hole with freezer tape, put aluminum foil over the container and then snap on the lid.

Save your bread wrappers, then "double bag" them for extra freezer protection, fill and close with a twistee.

FRESH FRUIT

For each 1 cup of cut-up fresh fruit, you can use 1 10 oz. pkg. frozen fruit, 1 cup frozen loose-pack fruit, or 1 c well-drained canned fruit. You may have to decrease the sugar called for in the fresh fruit recipe by about 1/3 cup. Remember these are all alternates for each other.

When you're out of ...

FRUIT RIPENING BOWL

Punch holes every few inches in a plastic bag, then place unripened fruit inside. Keep at room temperature. The holes are necessary to let air circulate, and the bag keeps in the odorless ethylene gas which fruits produce for the ripening process.

GARLIC, FRESH

You can use 1/8 t minced dried garlic or 1/8 t garlic powder for each clove.

If all you have is garlic salt, try about 1/4 t and omit salt in the recipe. Taste, then add more garlic salt and/or regular salt to your taste.

GARLIC SALT

Cut a good-sized clove of garlic in half. Pour into a shaker jar with a lid (like some spices come in — or the garlic salt you're out of.) Add salt and a few grains of rice. Pretty pungent at first (go easy), but tames down.

GELATIN, FLAVORED, PACKAGED

Make your own — from any leftover fruit juice, or combination.

SS LC▶   HOMEMADE GELATIN DESSERT

      1 envelope unflavored gelatin or 1 T bulk
      1/4 c cold water
      2 T sugar
      3/4 c boiling water
      1 c fruit juice
      Flavoring, if desired
      Food coloring, dropped from end of toothpick

Sprinkle gelatin over cold water in bowl to soften. Stir in sugar, and boiling water until gelatin is dissolved.

Add fruit juice such as pineapple, orange, apricot or peach nectar, cranberry or grapefruit. Chill until partially set. Add 1 cup diced fruit. Stir gently. Chill until set.

GRAPE JUICE FOR JELLY

GRAPE-BEET JELLY

Save some of the juice when canning or eating beets. (Just freeze small amounts until you've accumulated three cups, then try this.)

3 c beet juice	4 c sugar
1 pkg. jelling powder	2 pkg. grape-flavored
	soft-drink mix, unsweetened

Mix together beet juice and jelling powder. Bring to a boil. Add sugar and dry drink mix. Stir thoroughly; bring to rolling boil and boil for five minutes. Skim, then pour into heated jelly glasses or jars. Seal with paraffin or lids.

GRAVY

EASY GRAVY

Need some for a special recipe, or there weren't quite enough meat juices in the roasting pan? A couple of bouillon cubes can help you out.

2 t (or 2 cubes) bouillon	2 T cornstarch
2 c boiling water	1/3 c cold water

Mix bouillon with boiling water in saucepan. Stir cornstarch into cold water; then add slowly to bouillon. Simmer until thickened.

GRAVY "BROWNER" (bottled)

Brown flour in drippings before adding liquid.

Add your salt to the flour first, before browning for gravy, to prevent lumps.

OR:

If you shake your flour in a tightly covered jar with water, drippings or milk, and your gravy is too pale, add 1/2 teaspoon instant coffee (won't affect the taste), or add a tablespoon of strong brewed coffee.

OR:

Leave out the salt, and add a tablespoon or so of soy sauce. Adds flavor as well as color.

When you're out of ...

GRAHAM FLOUR

Substitute whole wheat flour, cup for cup

HAM

LF▶ *It's a pea-soup day and you have green or yellow peas and not a bit of ham for flavoring. That's when a can of chicken broth and bacon bits (bacon subsitute) can save the day (or soup?).*

Use your usual recipe for making the soup, adding broth and bacon bits instead of ham.

It's an ideal soup for those low fat diets as well. Use the bacon bits with care as they are salty. Taste before adding salt, if any.

OR:

Fry some lean bacon ends (chopped), drain off fat, and use as above, instead of bacon substitute.

HAMBURGER, FOR SPAGHETTI SAUCE

Use a cup or so of any left over meat, canned chunk chicken or even an inexpensive chicken sandwich spread. Add to the sauteed onions and seasoned tomato sauce.

OR:

Try about 6 slices of bacon (bacon ends are cheaper). Fry bacon until cooked, but still limp. Remove bacon and cut into strips (about 1/4 inch). Drain off fat from pan, return bacon, add tomato sauce and seasonings and simmer a few minutes. Add grated cheddar cheese just before stirring in cooked spaghetti.

OR:

See MOCK MEATBALLS, page 10.

HAM, PORK, BACON FOR BAKED BEANS

Not a smidgeon of meat to put in the beans? Try a teaspoon of smoke flavoring and no one will ever know.

To make these a complete protein (see page 51) add 1/2 cup or so of seeds or nuts. Or serve with cornbread or whole wheat bread.

HERBS, FRESH

Use 1 teaspoon crushed dried herbs or 1/2 teaspoon ground herbs for each tablespoon fresh herbs.

When you're out of ...

HONEY

For 1 cup, use 1 1/4 cups sugar, and increase liquid by 1/4 cup. Sugar may be brown or white. For some delicately balanced recipes you may be taking a chance on the texture.

HONEY, LIQUID

If your honey has started to "sugar", place jar in hot water and bring the water to a boil. Turn off the heat and let the honey stand in hot water until liquid again.

Micro≈ Be sure honey is in a microwave-safe container. Remove lid, then heat for about 10 seconds, or until honey is liquid.

ICE CREAM, FOR MILKSHAKES

Try this icy cold, refreshing drink at half the cost.

PUDDING SHAKES

3 c ice cubes
1 c non-fat instant
  milk powder

1 pkg. instant pudding
  (any flavor)

Put ice cubes into blender, then pour in water to the 3 cup mark. Add powdered milk and instant pudding. Blend slowly until ingredients are mixed, then whirl on highest speed for a minute or two, until ice is completely melted for a nice creamy texture. Pour into glasses and let stand in the refrigerator a few minutes. Serve with a straw or a spoon.

OR:

Another hot weather drink that can take the place of a milkshake is:

SS▶   FRUIT SMOOTHIE

For each serving use about 1/2 cup *frozen* fruit (any kind will do, but bananas and berries are especially delicious). Put whole berries (cut other fruit into chunks) into blender. Pour in about 3/4 c milk — enough so the fruit just begins to float. Add 1/2 teaspoon vanilla, 1 teaspoon of sugar (or sugar substitute) and whirl until frothy. The frozen fruit freezes the milk so you have a nice thick drink.

BONUS HINT: Did you know that when bananas get a bit too soft for pleasant eating, you can peel, wrap in plastic wrap and freeze them? They slice while still frozen.

When you're out of ...

ICE CUBE TRAYS

Use plastic foam egg containers (not the paper mache kind). Discard the lid and fill the compartments with water, punch mix, or fruit juice, and freeze. You'll get prettily shaped cubes.

JAM

This is the easiest to make, best tasting jam ever. It does need to be refrigerated and must be frozen if kept over a couple of weeks.

                        BERRY JAM

    1 pound frozen berries — any kind: black, blue,
    boysen, straw ...
       or 4 cups of fresh
    1 small pkg. lemon flavored gelatin (can be sugar free)
       or compatible or same flavor gelatin

Heat berries until almost boiling. This may be done in a 4 cup glass measure in the microwave. Will take 4 to 6 minutes.
Or may be heated on the stove — about the same amount of time.
If using regular gelatin, sprinkle over berries and return to microwave or stove. Heat for a minute or two until gelatin is dissolved.
If using sugar-free gelatin, sprinkle over berries, but do **not** heat, just stir to dissolve.
Cool, then refrigerate until firm. Takes about an hour to thicken.
You may add extra sugar or sugar substitute if not quite sweet enough for your taste.

OR:

Here's a tasty way to use up zucchini and fill up your jam shelf at the same time.

ZUCCHINI-PINEAPPLE-APRICOT JAM

6 c zucchini	1 c (20 oz.) crushed pineapple
1 c water	2 pkg. (3 oz.) or 1 pkg. (6 oz.)
6 c sugar	apricot-flavored gelatin
	2 T lemon juice

Use fairly large zucchini — peel, cut in small pieces and puree in blender. Put zucchini in large saucepan; add water; bring to boil and simmer for 6 minutes. Add sugar, lemon juice, and well-drained pineapple and cook 6 minutes more. Add apricot-flavored gelatin and cook another 6 minutes. Seal with paraffin in jelly glasses or in canning jars with lids. Makes about 4 pints of jam.

OR:

If you just want something to spread on your toast right now, try thick applesauce with a sprinkle of sugar and cinnamon — adding a slice of American cheese (those pre-cut squares) gives an "apple-pie-with-cheese" taste. Or slice a ripe banana right onto your toast and smash with a fork, or do the same with any well-drained canned fruit — sugar to taste. Don't need the sweets? A ripe avocado handled the same way, sprinkled with a little lemon juice, is a real breakfast treat.

OR:

Did you know that you can make strawberry jam from frozen berries, with no cooking? Here's how:

SS LC▶   FROZEN STRAWBERRY JAM

2 pkgs. (12 oz. each) frozen strawberries*
3 1/2 c sugar (or 1 cup sugar substitute)
1/2 bottle liquid fruit pectin

Stir sugar into thawed, mashed strawberries until well mixed. Let stand, stirring occasionally for 20 minutes. Be sure sugar has dissolved completely, then add pectin and stir for three minutes.

Pour into jelly glasses (or freezer containers, if you want to keep the jam for over six weeks). Let stand, covered, about 24 hours, or until set. Seal with paraffin.

Keep in refrigerator, or freeze. This jam is a bit thinner than regular cooked jam, and thins even more if stirred when serving. If this happens — serve it on pancakes or waffles!

*Be sure to get those frozen without sugar.

When you're out of ...

KETCHUP OR CATSUP

If you need the catsup for cooked mixtures, just combine the ingredients below and add to your recipe in place of catsup. However, if you need to use it as a garnish — on hot dogs, for example, follow the directions for thickening.

1 (8 oz.) can tomato sauce	dash of cinnamon
1/4 c sugar	1 T vinegar

Pour the tomato sauce into a small sauce pan, and then just boil away some of the water until it begins to thicken. Now add the other ingredients and simmer for 3 or 4 minutes more.

LEMON, FOR TEA

An old-fashioned lemon drop dropped in your tea is a good "in place of" and lightly sweetens the tea, too.

LEMONS, FRESH

Lemons a bit shriveled or hard? Soak overnight in cold water to plump 'em.

Out of lemons, lemon juice, or lemon extract? A dash of lemon drink mix powder works great.

LEMON JUICE

Unless you need the flavor of lemon, you can substitute white vinegar.

If you have a lot of lemons, prepare for the day when you'll be out of them. Freeze in ice-cube trays (juice and pulp). When you're ready for lemonade, plop a few cubes into a glass, add water, ice cubes and sugar (or sugar substitute) to taste.

You can add one lemon cube to a glass of ice tea.

LEMON PEPPER

1 T grated lemon peel, dried	2 T salt (coarse, if possible)
6 T coarse black pepper	1 t garlic powder

Dry the grated peel thoroughly in 150° oven, or sun dry for several days. Then mix all ingredients together and put in a bottle with a shaker top.

When you're out of ...

LUCK

The salt shaker poured too freely, and you ended up with a super salty salad? Add a scant teaspoon of sugar — no sugary taste, just tones down the salt, and enhances the flavor. Remember, this only cuts down the salty taste, not the salt content (for those of you on low-salt diets.)

OR:
If it's a stew or other cooked concoction you've over-salted, put in a medium-size peeled potato, cook awhile longer, and the potato will absorb the excess salt.

OR:
Never tell people what you are making for dessert and always keep vanilla ice cream in the freezer. Many disasters topped with ice cream can be called "Cherry Delight" or some such "cute" name.

OR:
Separating an egg to beat the whites high and fluffy, and a bit of yolk drops in? Use one of the half egg shells to scoop it out easily.
Speaking of eggs ... have you ever mixed unpeeled hard boiled with fresh eggs, and hated to crack them to find out which they were? Here's an easy trick — spin 'em. The hard boiled will spin fast and easily, and the fresh ones will lumber around. Explanation: the yolk inside the uncooked ones puts them off balance, and they won't twirl.

OR:
When the toast is burned beyond scraping, wrap and put in the freezer to save for the next time you're making meat loaf. Add onions and garlic (or garlic powder); crumble up a slice or two of the burned toast; and you get a smokey-barbecue flavor.

OR:
CAUTION: *Do not use the hint below with any glass utensil —ONLY METAL pans. The sudden change in temperature may explode glass.*
Something distracted you, and that concoction you were so carefully watching sticks and burns? Save the good food by doing this.

Immediately put an inch or so of cold water in a large pan, or in the sink and set the pan with the burned food in it. Let stand for a few minutes. Carefully spoon out the unburned portion. There will be no burned taste, and the scorched portion will come off with little scrubbing. This works even if you've let the water boil away from vegetables or fruit, and a few pieces on the bottom get black.

When you're out of ...

MARSHMALLOW CREME

You'll never believe how one egg white and the other ingredients balloon up into a quart of taste-alike, use-alike

HOMEMADE MARSHMALLOW CREME

White of one large egg	1 c powdered sugar
1 c clear corn syrup	1 t vanilla

In large mixer bowl beat egg whites until foamy. Pour syrup in a steady stream over egg white, beating constantly at high speed. Continue beating for 10 to 15 minutes. Add sugar and vanilla. Beat until smooth. Makes approximately one quart. Store in refrigerator.

Test your homemade creme in this white fudge dotted with chocolate bits.

FRECKLE-FACED FUDGE

2 c sugar	1 t vanilla
1 c milk	1/2 c marshmallow creme
1/2 t salt	1/3 c chocolate bits
1 T butter or margarine	

Butter the sides of a large, heavy saucepan. (This keeps the sugar from crystallizing.) Combine sugar, milk and salt in the buttered pan. Stir, while cooking over medium heat, until sugar dissolves. Then cook to softball stage (238°) with no stirring unless absolutely necessary.

Remove from heat and put the butter on top — do not stir. Cool to lukewarm, then stir in the by-now-melted butter and vanilla. Beat until candy just begins to hold its shape; then quickly stir in marshmallow creme. Beat until thick. Spread in buttered pan. Press chocolate bits (point-side down) into the still-warm fudge and mark off into squares. Cut when cold.

When you're out of ...

MAYONNAISE

Make your own:

EASY MAYONNAISE

1 egg
1/2 t garlic salt
    (or regular salt)
1 T lemon juice
1 t dry mustard

1 c oil
Dill or other herb,
    to your taste, optional

In blender whirl first four ingredients together with 1/4 c oil, for a few seconds. Then add rest of oil slowly (with blender running). Keep refrigerated.

No blender? Beat first four ingredients and 1/4 c oil with hand beater or mixer. With mixer, pour oil slowly with mixer at medium speed. With hand beater, find a friend to pour, or stop and add about 1/8 c (2 T) at a time, and continue beating after each addition.

MAYONNAISE, ENOUGH

Just add all the dribbles and drops in your salad dressing bottles to the almost-empty mayonnaise jar. Shake well. French, Russian, Onion or Chive dressing adds a delightful taste to potato salad.

When you're out of ...

AP▶ MEAT

To help you expand your ability to replace animal porteins with plant proteins, there are a few facts that will help.

Proteins are made of twenty-two amino acids which must be linked together in a chain to form the nutrient which your body needs. Of these 22, nine cannot be made by your body, and must come from the food you eat. These nine essential amino acids are contained in meat, fish, poultry, eggs and milk products (complete proteins).

However, plant proteins (incomplete proteins) are lacking in one or more of these nine essentials — but by combining plant sources that complement each other, you can be sure of forming that important *complete* chain. When any of the links are missing, the chain is useless and you've lost the protein nutrients.

Just be sure you include (at any one meal) foods from two of the groups below. Suggested amounts per serving are: Group A — 3/4 to 1 cup, Group B — 1/2 cup, Group C — nuts, 2 tablespoons; seeds, 3 to 4 tablespoons.

Group A	Group B	Group C
LEGUMES	GRAINS	NUTS
Dry beans	Barley	Almonds
Any variety,	Bulgar	Cashews
including limas,	Corn	Coconut
garbanzos, mung	Oats	Peanuts
Dry peas	Rice	Pecans
(green & yellow)	Rye	Pinenuts
Peanuts	Wheat	Pistachio
Lentils	Pasta	Walnuts
Soybeans		SEEDS
		Sesame
		Sunflower

Examples:
Peanut butter and whole wheat bread (A and B)
Split pea and barley soup (A and B)
Whole wheat muffins with chopped nuts (B and C)
Baked beans with cornbread (A and B)

When you're replacing meat (including poultry and fish) with other animal proteins such as milk products (milk, cheese, yogurt, cottage cheese) or eggs, you are serving complete proteins, so you don't have to worry about combinations.

However, when you want to stretch a small amount of meat, enhance your protein intake with any of the foods from Groups A, B, or C.

For hearty lunches or light suppers try some of these meat savers.

AP▶ <h2 style="text-align:center">BEANY BURRITOS</h2>

> 2 cans refried beans (or mash your own leftover chili beans)
> Chili powder, cumin, hot sauce to taste
> Cheddar cheese (about one cup)
> Small onion, chopped
> 8 tortillas

Heat beans and seasonings in double boiler until hot. Meanwhile grate the cheese and chop the onion. Heat the tortillas in a dry frying pan over medium heat, one by one. Peek underneath, and when brown spots appear, flip to the other side, until that side becomes slightly browned. Place tortilla on a plate, sprinkle with onions and cheese and two or three serving-size spoons of beans. Fold up the ends, roll and serve.

OR:
Try this for a French and Mexican combination!

AP▶ <h2 style="text-align:center">CHILI RELLENO SANDWICH</h2>

> 1 or 2 cans green chili peppers   Sliced day-old bread
> Monterey Jack cheese   Eggs and milk

Can't give you quantities because it depends on how many "French toast" sandwiches you're going to make.

Place a thick layer of chilis on a slice of bread, then a thick slice of cheese, and cover with another slice of bread. Dip both sides of the sandwich in egg and milk mixture (about a tablespoon of milk per egg, whipped together with a fork in a shallow pan). Fry in a little butter or margarine until cheese melts. Need a fork with these!

OR:
Tomato soup and bacon team with eggplant for a quick oven dish.

AP▶ <h2 style="text-align:center">EGGPLANT CASSEROLE</h2>

> 2 medium eggplants   1 medium onion
> 4 slices bacon   1 can condensed tomato soup
> 1 c cheese

Peel and cube eggplants; cook in just enough water to cover for 10 minutes; drain well. Cut up bacon and saute with onion; then add eggplant, condensed soup and cheese. Mix well — put in greased casserole and top with bread crumbs tossed with grated cheese. Bake at 350° for 15 to 20 minutes.

MEAT (cont.)

OR:

You can make some tasty protein dishes with dried beans, nuts, or cheese taking the place of meat. Here are some salads to try:

APPLE CHEESE SALAD

1 pkg. lemon-flavored gelatin	1 large eating apple
2 c hot water	(red or golden delicious)
1 t salt	1 three-ounce pkg. cream
1 t sugar	cheese
2 T lemon juice	1 c walnuts (chopped coarsely)

If you want a fancy molded salad: Dissolve gelatin in hot water. Add salt, sugar and lemon juice. Pour half of gelatin mixture into 1-quart mold (a 9x4x3 1/2-inch bread pan makes a good mold). Core apple and cut into 1/4 inch crosswise slices. Cut three slices in half; and remaining apple into small wedge-shaped pieces. When gelatin in mold is firm, arrange half apple slices on top of gelatin. Beat remaining plain gelatin until fluffy, then fold in remaining apple, cheese and nuts. Spread over gelatin-apple layer. Chill until firm.

If you want an easier version: Make your gelatin mixture, beat when syrupy, then fold in chopped apples, cheese and nuts. Pour in 8x8 inch pan and cut in squares when firm.

Serve with peanut butter filled celery sticks (for extra protein).

OR:
AP▶   TACO-ISH SALAD

1 medium head iceberg lettuce, shredded	1 c coarsely crushed taco chips
2 cans (15 oz. ea) chili with beans	1/2 c olives (stuffed or black), thinly sliced
1/2 c chopped onion	1 c shredded Monterey Jack
1 c diced tomatoes	or cheddar cheese

Heat chili, then spoon over rest of lettuce in shallow serving bowl. Sprinkle chili with remaining ingredients and toss lightly. Or you can put the "tossing ingredients" into separate bowls, to be mixed to taste. Serve with Italian dressing and/or cream cheese.

AP▶ MACBEAN SALAD

1 pkg. (8 oz. elbow macaroni, cooked)	2 T cider vinegar
1 can (about 16 oz.) kidney beans, drained	1 c mayonnaise or salad dressing
3 medium carrots, grated	1 1/2 t seasoned salt
1 1/2 c chopped celery	1/4 t pepper
1/4 c chopped parsley	Romaine or other lettuce
	2 large tomatoes, sliced

Combine first five ingredients in a large bowl. In a small bowl, mix together vinegar, mayonnaise, salt and pepper; beat until blended; fold into macaroni mixture. Chill at least an hour.

Line a salad bowl with lettuce, spoon macaroni mixture in center. Place tomato slices around edge.

OR:

Tofu is growing in popularity with nutritionists because of its protein value, and low-calorie content.

Tofu is soybean curd, a complete protein, and fat free. It is now found in larger super markets — sometimes in the cold produce sections (with bean sprouts, etc.) or in the refrigerated area. It's bland taste absorbs flavors. Try it! You'll be pleasantly surprised.

AP▶ EGGY TOFU SALAD

1 lb. tofu, cubed	1/8 t dill
2 T dry mustard	2 hard-cooked eggs, chopped
1/4 t garlic powder	1/2 c chopped celery
2 T chopped green onions	Salt and pepper to taste

Combine ingredients and mix thoroughly, then chill. Serve on bed of chopped lettuce.

OR:
AP▶ MOCK POTATO SALAD

1 1/2 c cauliflowerets	6 hard-cooked eggs, chopped
1 c diced celery	3 T mayonnaise
4 green onions, chopped	8 oz. tofu, cut in cubes

Combine vegetables with eggs and mix with mayonnaise. Add salt and pepper to taste. Fold in tofu. Refrigerate before serving.

MEAT (cont.)

Tofu also combines well with cooked vegetables.

AP▶   TOFU VEGETABLE SCRAMBLE

> 1 c sliced vegetables (combinations are better)
> (green pepper, green onion, green beans, thinly sliced
> carrots, zucchini, whatever — or use one cup of any
> leftover vegetables)
> 2 eggs, fork-beaten with salt, pepper, garlic powder
> 8 oz. Tofu, crumbled

If using fresh vegetables, stir-fry until crisp tender. With cooked vegetables, heat in small amount of water. When vegetables are hot, add seasoned eggs, then tofu. Cook just until set.

OR:
Here's a different kind of meatless dish, with cornmeal helping with the protein content.

AP▶   POLENTA

1/3 c oil	3 c drained cooked tomatoes
2 medium onions	1/2 c button or chopped
1 large clove garlic	mushrooms
4 or 5 sprigs parsley	2 c corn meal
2 1/2 t salt (divided)	2 qts. boiling water
1/8 t thyme	1 c grated cheese
1/8 t sage	(American or Cheddar)

Brown onions, garlic, parsley, 1 t salt and spices in oil. Add tomatoes and simmer for 30 minutes, stirring occasionally. Add mushrooms and return to simmer.

While the sauce is simmering, stir corn meal gradually into boiling water, with remaining 1 1/2 t salt added. Cook until thick, stirring often.

Spread half the corn meal on heated platter. Cover with half the sauce and cheese. Top with rest of corn meal, then sauce and cheese. Serve immediately.

MEAT (cont.)

When unexpected company drops in and you don't have any meat or chicken left from Sunday's dinner, surprise them with this easy to prepare and delicious

AP▶   SUNDAY SUPPER PIE

1/2 c cooked macaroni   1 c Cheddar cheese, cubed
1 c milk   1 t onion, minced
1 c cubed day-old bread   3 eggs, well-beaten
1/4 c margarine, melted   1/2 t salt
1 can (10 oz.) cream of mushroom soup, undiluted

Stir everything together and pour into a greased 3-quart casserole. Bake at 350° for 45 minutes.

OR:

This takes a little effort, but well worth it.

AP▶   CHEESE CABBAGE ROLLS

1 c cooked rice   1/4 c finely cut parsley
1 to 2 c grated Cheddar or   6 large outside cabbage leaves
  American cheese*   1 can condensed mushroom,
1/4 t salt   or tomato soup
1/4 t pepper   2 T finely diced pimiento
1/4 t paprika   (optional)

Mix together rice, 1 c cheese, seasonings and parsley. Cook cabbage leaves in rapidly boiling water to cover for 2 minutes, or until limp. Drain well. Spread rice mixture on leaves. Fold over ends and roll into small package. Place rolls in baking dish; pour condensed soup over all; cover and bake 30 minutes in 350° oven.

*May sprinkle 1 c grated cheese over top for last 10 minutes of baking.

Micro≈ Steam cabbage leaves in covered dish with 1/2 c water for 5 or 6 minutes, until limp. Mix filling, and place over heavy vein at base of leaf, fold over sides and roll. Place in a ring in a 10-inch pie plate, pour over condensed soup, cover and micro for 10 to 12 minutes. Sprinkle extra cheese over top after removing from oven, if desired.

CHILI PEPPER "QUICHE"

3 eggs	2 cans green chilis (4 oz. each)
1 c milk	2 to 3 medium tomatoes
1/2 c biscuit mix	(about 2 cups)
1/2 t salt	2 c shredded Cheddar cheese
	(about 1/2 lb.)

Beat first four ingredients together until foamy. Remove stems and seeds from chilies, rinse and place in 8x8 baking dish, greased. Top with tomatoes; sprinkle with cheese. Pour egg mixture over vegetables. Bake uncovered 40 to 45 minutes in 350° oven.

When you're out of ...

MEAT, ENOUGH

Do yourself a favor, and discover Chinese cooking. The Chinese can stretch 1/2 lb. of meat into tasty concoctions to serve 4 or more, increasing the protein with bean sprouts, eggs, tofu, etc.
Here is one example.

PORK TOFU SOUP

6 c chicken broth	3 T soy sauce
1/2 lb. boneless pork loin	1 T minced fresh ginger root
or 1 c leftover pork roast	1 T cornstarch, mixed with
3 c thinly sliced green	2 T cold water
cabbage (or Chinese	1/2 lb. Tofu, cut into
cabbage)	thin strips
1/2 c sliced mushrooms	1/2 c white vinegar
1/2 c sliced green onions	1 t pepper
1/2 c drained sliced	2 eggs, fork-whipped
bamboo shoots	

In large saucepan bring broth to boil. Add ingredients, through ginger root. When mixture boils again, stir in cornstarch mixture. Boil 3 minutes, add tofu strips, vinegar and pepper. Pour eggs in a steady stream into the soup and stir once. About 4 to 6 servings.

MILK, FRESH

Use 1/2 cup *each* evaporated milk and water for each cup needed.

OR:
Use 1/3 cup instant nonfat dry milk plus one cup water, minus 1 tablespoon.

OR:

A▶ You'll be amazed at the results if you use any carbonated beverage such as ginger ale or club soda in any of your baked goodies. Also makes light and fluffy pancakes and waffles.

OR:

LF▶ To add hot milk to boiled potatoes before mashing, add instant powdered milk to the hot, drained potato water in the quantity needed, using measurements on the milk package. Vitamins otherwise lost in the water will be saved.

OR:

A▶ Replace all or part of the milk in most any recipe with non-dairy creamer, mixed one-to-one with boiling water, or use less creamer for a less rich solution.

A note of caution: If using non-dairy creamer in baking, remember to cut back the shortening in the recipe, as the creamers are mostly vegetable oil based.

OR:

All set to make fudge and you discover the children have drunk all the milk? Substitute coffee for the milk, and make MOCHA FUDGE.

OR:

A▶ Put peeled and seeded zucchini chunks in blender on medium for 45 seconds. Use same amount as milk called for in baked goods, meat loaf, etc. Makes cakes super moist.

When you're out of ...

MILK, SWEETENED CONDENSED

HOMEMADE CONDENSED MILK

1 c instant nonfat dry milk	1/3 c boiling water
2/3 c sugar	3 T butter or margarine, melted

Combine all ingredients in blender and whirl until smooth. Makes about the same amount as one can of condensed milk.

OR:

If you don't have a blender, here's another version.

Combine 1 cup plus 2 tablespoons nonfat dry milk with 1/2 cup warm water, mixing well. Set in pan of hot water and stir in 3/4 cup granulated sugar, stirring until sugar is dissolved. This also equals one can of condensed milk. Use in any recipe calling for sweetened condensed milk.

When you're out of ...

MOLASSES

When you eat this gingerbread, remember that in the early Nineteenth Century it was known as White Ginger Cake (or Bread) and highly prized because it was made without molasses. It was special because sugar was expensive and hard to get, and people were tired of molasses flavor — often the only available sweetener.

MOLASSES-LESS GINGERBREAD

1 c butter or margarine	3/4 t cinnamon
1 1/4 c brown sugar	1 1/2 t ground ginger
2 eggs	1/2 t nutmeg
2 c sifted flour	1 t vinegar
1 t baking soda	1 c milk
3/4 t salt	

Preheat oven to 350°. Grease and flour 8x8x2-inch pan.

Cream butter or margarine. Add brown sugar gradually, creaming thoroughly. Add eggs and beat well. Sift dry ingredients. Blend vinegar with milk and add alternately with dry ingredients to the brown sugar mixture. Bake for 1 hour. Serve warm or cool.

OR:

To make GINGERBREAD COOKIES — increase flour by 3/4 cup and omit milk. Chill dough for an hour or so, then roll on well-floured board, 1/4 inch thick. Cut shapes with cookie cutters. Bake on greased cookie sheet in 375° oven for 10-12 minutes. Decorate when cool.

When you're out of ...

MOZZARELLA CHEESE

Use Monterey Jack — just as tasty though not quite as "stringy" and cheaper

NOODLES

Try making your own.

HOMEMADE NOODLES

1 egg
3/4 sifted flour
1/2 t salt

Mix egg with flour and salt — makes a very stiff dough. Add more flour if necessary. Roll as thin as possible on well-floured board. Cut into small triangles or squares and drop a few at a time into boiling broth or stew, and cook 20 minutes.

If you prefer the noodles in narrow strips here's how to make the cutting easier. Drape a bath towel over the back of a straight-backed chair. Roll the noodle dough into a rectangle about 1/16 inch thick. Place over the towel to air-dry for about 20 minutes, (the dough becomes stiffer, but is still flexible). Put dough back on the cutting board and fold in half, then in half again, and again until you have a long, narrow rectangle about three inches wide. Now cut through all layers, whatever width you wish. These fresh noodles should be cooked within 2 or 3 days.

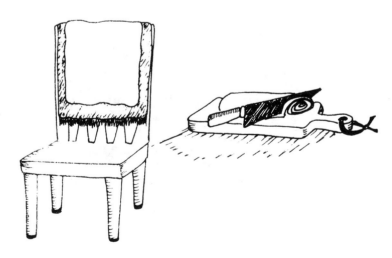

When you're out of ...

NOODLES, FOR CHOW MEIN

If you forgot to pick up Chinese noodles for that Chinese dinner you'd planned, spaghetti can be a surprise substitute.

FAKE CHINESE NOODLES

Cook spaghetti*, rinse and drain. Shake in a bag with a couple of tablespoons of cornstarch. For CRISPY NOODLES, heat about 1/4 inch of oil in a frying pan. Make sure the oil is hot enough to crisp and lightly brown a small piece of spaghetti in a minute. Have the spaghetti cut into two-inch lengths, and cook a handful at a time. Drain on paper towels.

For pan-fried noodles, cover the bottom of a frying pan with oil. Leave the spaghetti uncut, and spread in the pan in four-inch circles. Fry crisply on one side, then serve — topped with your favorite chow mein vegetable and meat mixture.

*Leftover spaghetti may be used, but be sure you bring it to room temperature before frying. Cold spaghetti tends to get hard, rather than crisp.

BONUS HINT: The CRISPY NOODLES make wonderful snacks when drained, then sprinkled with grated parmesan cheese, garlic salt or seasoning salt.

NOODLES, LASAGNA

Slice fresh zucchini into 1/4 inch lengthwise slices. Use the raw slices in place of the wide noodles in your favorite lasagna recipe.

NUTS

For the crunch of nuts without the expense, try browning oatmeal in a 400° oven. Spread the oatmeal evenly on a cookie sheet, and stir once or twice. Takes about 20 minutes. You can start with a small amount of margarine, but it's not necessary.

If you have a few nuts — put in about 1/4 of what the recipe calls for and make up the difference with toasted oatmeal. Now you've got the flavor as well as the crunch and saved money besides.

OR:
Crushed cornflakes are an excellent substitute.

OR:
No nuts for brownies or cake? Add 1/2 to 1 teaspoon black walnut flavoring for a nutty taste.

OR:
Use grapenuts cereal as a substitute for nuts. Just as crunchy and adds extra nutrition. Great as a topping for (or in) brownies.

OR:
Substitute wheat germ for nuts in a carrot cake or any other labeled goodie.

When you're out of ...

NUTS, ENOUGH

When grated or crushed nuts are called for in a recipe and you haven't quite enough — substitute coarsely crushed graham cracker crumbs.

OIL, FOR SAUTEING

Use bottled salad dressing, such as Italian, Golden Caesar, or any other oil-based type. The vinegar tenderizes the meat, and the herbs and spices add a unique flavor.

OR:
Also good for stir-frying vegetables.

ONIONS, FRESH

Use 1 T minced dried onion or 1 t onion powder. If you have only onion salt, eliminate the salt in the recipe and try 1 t onion salt at a time until you reach the flavor desired.

ONIONS, SWEET

To turn strong tasting yellow onions into mild sweet ones; slice onions thinly into a bowl and pour boiling water over them. Drain and chill. They will be crisp and almost as mild as the big sweet Spanish onions.

When you're out of ...

OLIVE OIL

If you enjoy the flavor of olive oil and feel it is too expensive to buy —try this: Soak four large green olives (unstuffed) in a cup of oil in a tightly covered glass jar for one week. You may leave the olives in the oil until it's all used up.

ORANGES

For two medium oranges use an 11 ounce can of drained mandarin orange sections. This will have a different taste, but still "citrusy".

ORANGES OR JUICE FOR GLAZING HAM

1/2 cube margarine or butter   1 T mustard
1 small package of orange gelatin

Melt butter, dissolve gelatin in it, after removing from heat. Stir until well dissolved, then blend in mustard and pour over ham

OVEN ROOM

When the oven is stuffed and you want warm rolls for dinner, wrap rolls in aluminum foil and heat in electric frying pan at 300° for 5 to 10 minutes.

PECANS

PECAN-LESS PIE

When you have the urge for a taste of Pecan Pie and haven't a nut in the house, use slightly crushed cornflakes in your favorite recipe. They will rise when baking and give a great flavor and a crunchy surface to the pie.

When you're out of ...

PIMENTOS

This is a neat trick for decorating cooked chicken or to use in Chicken a la King. Cut slivers of bright red tomatoes (no pulp) and add to foods just before serving.

POPCORN SALT

Pour regular salt into blender. Set at medium-high speed, then switch on and off several times for a minute or two. The salt will be so fine that it will stick to popcorn, french fries, or nuts, instead of sliding off into the bottom of the bowl.

POTATOES

Want to make Potato Salad and find that you are out of potatoes? Or you haven't time to cook and cool them? Use frozen french fries in this recipe or your own favorite.

'SPECIALLY GOOD POTATO SALAD

2 pkg. (10 oz. ea.) of frozen french fries	2 T parsley, chopped
	1 c mayonnaise
2/3 c diced cucumbers	1 1/2 t salt
2/3 c sliced radishes	1/2 t pepper
1/3 c onions, chopped	2 eggs, hard-cooked, chopped
3/4 c celery, diced	1 egg, hard-cooked, sliced
1/4 c sweet pickle relish	

Put frozen french fried potatoes into 2 cups boiling water. Cover, remove from heat and let stand for 5 minutes. Pour off water and drain potatoes on paper towels. Cut into cubes and combine with above ingredients. Decorate top of salad with egg slices. Chill.

OR:
Another good use of frozen french fries is for:

EASY SCALLOPED POTATOES

1 (10 oz.) pkg. frozen french fries*
Thin White Sauce (follow the recipe on page 22)
    increasing ONLY the milk to 3 cups)
2 T minced onion   Salt and pepper to taste

Layer 1/2 of the fries in a 9x13 baking dish; sprinkle with 1/2
of the onions, then pour over 1/2 of the sauce. Repeat layers. Cover
and bake for about one hour in a 350° oven.
For extra protein you might add shredded cheese to the white sauce,
or make SCALLOPED HAM AND POTATOES by adding a cup of
diced ham (1/2 cup at a time) when you put in the onions. * Can use
frozen hash browns instead.

Micro≈ Make white sauce recipe on page 22, but **do not** increase
milk. Now follow directions above and microwave for 6 to 8 minutes,
stirring twice. Let stand, covered, to thicken.
Shredded cheese, if used, should be stirred in during the last two or
three minutes of cooking.

When you're out of ...

PUMPKIN FOR PIES

Simply use any yellow winter squash, carrots, sweet potatoes, or
yams. The vegetables may be fresh cooked or canned. Mash before
using in your favorite pumpkin pie recipe. You may want to increase
the sugar a bit.

QUICK MIX FOR BISCUITS, PANCAKES, WAFFLES

Do as they did in the "good old days" — make 'em from scratch. Here are biscuits that free you from the tedium of cutting in the shortening, fast and easy pancakes and waffles without having to fold in egg whites.

SALAD OIL BISCUITS

1 3/4 c all-purpose flour	3 T salad oil
3 t baking powder	2/3 c milk
1/2 t salt	

Preheat oven to 450°. Measure dry ingredients and sift into a bowl. Pour oil and milk into measuring cup (do not mix), and pour all at once into the dry ingredients. Stir just until mixture clings together in a ball.

Knead on a lightly floured board about 12 times, until smooth. Pat or roll 1/2 inch thick and cut with a biscuit cutter. Bake until golden brown, 10 to 12 minutes.

EASY PANCAKES

1 c sifted flour	1 beaten egg
3 t baking powder	3/4 c milk
1 T sugar	2 T salad oil
1/2 t salt	

Sift together dry ingredients. Combine egg, milk, and salad oil. Add dry ingredients, beat with rotary beater just until moistened. Bake on hot griddle.

QUICKIE WAFFLES

2 eggs	2 c flour
1 1/2 c milk	4 t baking powder
1 T sugar	3/4 t salt
1/4 c salad oil	

Put eggs in mixer bowl, beat until fluffy; then add remaining ingredients and beat just until smooth. Pour onto preheated waffle iron.

RAISINS

Use your ingenuity and try cut-up dates, prunes, dried apricots, apples, figs, etc.

When you're out of ...

RECIPE CARDS

Pretty up your recipe box by cutting 3x5 cards from Christmas, birthday, anniversary cards; then paste recipe on back (or write it). Also helps as a reminder of favorite recipes for "birthday persons".

ROASTING RACK

Crisscross carrot and celery sticks to place meat or poultry on. Bonus —the gravy will be enhanced by the extra flavor.

OR:
Lay the number of old forks needed for the size of the roast — tines down — to keep the meat from sticking.

OR:
Peel six large onions and slice them in half; then place flat side down in the bottom of the roasting pan. Balance a turkey or roast on top of them and cook as usual. The onions will disintegrate but impart a nice flavor to the meat and gravy.

SAGE, POWDERED

When the recipe calls for sage, and you are lucky to have a plant of grey-green or blue sage in your garden, pick a few leaves and cut fine with scissors. Use 3 times as much fresh cut sage as powdered dry sage.

To make your own powdered dry sage; hose off the sage bushes; allow to dry (1-2 hours); then snip off a few lengths and tie in bouquets. Hang in airy room, hall or breezeway, until dry enough to crumble with fingers. Then put only the leaves (no stems) into the blender and whirl. Keep in an airtight bottle or jar.

Any leafy herb or spice may be treated as above. Several bottles of "home-cured" herbs make nice hostess gifts.

SALAD OIL FOR OIL AND VINEGAR DRESSING

Use buttermilk instead — you'll save on the calories and cholesterol. Doesn't thicken like a well-shaken oil and vinegar, but gives a good taste to coleslaw as well as tossed green salads.

SALT

Lemon and coarse ground or seasoned pepper will zing up salads, vegetables, fish or meats.

When you're out of ...

SALT, SEASONED

NO-SALT SEASONING

Measure one teaspoon each:

Onion powder
Horseradish powder
Cumin
Paprika
Parsley flakes, finely ground

Ground leaf thyme
Ground celery seed
Ground black pepper
Dry mustard
Garlic powder

Mix all ingredients together and store in a tightly covered jar. Use, with or without salt, on salads, vegetables, egg dishes, fish, or poultry. Makes 1/2 cup. Use sparingly, to taste.

SAUSAGE

Make your own from hamburger. For 2 1/2 pounds of meat use 1 1/2 teaspoons sage, 1/2 teaspoon marjoram, 2 teaspoons salt, 1 teaspoon pepper and 1/2 teaspoon nutmeg. Mix thoroughly and let stand overnight.

SHORTENING FOR PIE CRUST

Use salad oil with super results. Enough for a two-crust pie.

SALAD OIL PASTRY

1 3/4 c flour
3/4 t salt

1/2 c salad oil
3-4 T cold water

Sift together flour and salt. Measure salad oil and cold water in same cup but do not stir. Add all at once to dry mixture. Stir lightly with a fork. Form into two balls, flatten slightly.

Roll each piece of dough between two 12-inch squares of wax paper. (Dampen the table slightly so paper won't slip). Peel off top sheet, then flip dough over into pie plate. Ease gently into pie plate, then remove paper. Bake as usual for single or double crust.

OR:

Substitute butter or margarine and omit the salt.

OR:

Make a graham cracker crust. See page 95 for a low calorie recipe. You can also use any crushed cookies or dry cereal in place of graham crackers.

When you're out of ...

SHORTENING, MARGARINE OR BUTTER, MELTED

Use 1 cup minus 2 tablespoons of salad oil. If it's melted margarine or butter you're out of — use the salad oil (1 cup minus 2 tablespoons) and add 1/2 teaspoon salt.

OR:
Save chicken fat or bacon drippings.

SODA

Use 1 teaspoon of ground ginger in your next kettle of beans (no trace of a taste) to discourage the usual "pop-off" after eating beans. Also will not destroy nutrients as soda might.

No soda handy for refrigerator deodorizer? Use a couple of charcoal briquettes.

Did you know that you can substitute 4 teaspoons baking powder for 1 teaspoon soda?

SOUR CREAM, COMMERCIAL

For each cup of commercial sour cream, put 4 teaspoons vinegar or lemon juice in a measuring cup, then fill to 1 cup level with undiluted evaporated milk; half and half; or sweet whipping cream.

OR:
In blender, place 1 cup cottage cheese, 2 tablespoons milk and 1 teaspoon lemon juice. Whirl on medium low speed until smooth. Good for dips.

OR:
LF LC▶ Replace the sour cream in any recipe with same amount of plain yogurt. It works! Less calories, too.

TRY:
PARTY FRUIT SALAD

Use 5-6 cups of any fruit such as sliced bananas, oranges, pineapple chunks, cantaloupe or melon balls and 1 chopped red apple. Add 1 cup small marshmallows (optional). Stir in 1 cup pineapple (or any fruit) yogurt. Nuts or coconut may be added.

OR:
LF LC▶ When preparing Beef Stroganoff replace the sour cream with 1 can cream of mushroom soup and 1 soup can of milk. Not as zippy, but very tasty.

When you're out of ...

SPICES, SPECIFIC

Ever reach for a spice can and discover a smidgeon instead of the teaspoon you need? This list will help you improvise.

SPICE SUBSTITUTIONS

1 t allspice	1/2 t cinnamon plus 1/8 t cloves
1 t anise	1 t cardamom
Bay leaf, small	1 t marjoram, oregano, rosemary, sage or thyme
Caraway seeds	dill, poppy or sesame seeds
Cayenne, dash	Few drops of hot pepper sauce or 1 t chili
1/2 t celery seed	1 T finely chopped celery leaves
1/4 c cinnamon sugar	1/4 c sugar and 1 t cinnamon
1 T Italian seasoning	1/4 t *each* oregano, basil, thyme, rosemary, and dash of cayenne
1 t mace	1 t nutmeg, allspice or cinnamon
1 t dry mustard	1 T prepared mustard
2 t pumpkin pie spice	1 t cinnamon, 1/2 t ginger, 1/4 t cloves, 1/4 t nutmeg
1 t poultry seasoning	1/2 t ground sage, 1/2 t thyme, 1/2 t rosemary (optional)
1 t saffron	1/2 t turmeric
1 t savory	1/2 t thyme, plus 1/2 t sage
1/2 c soy sauce	3 T worcestershire sauce plus 1 T water

General hint: Use 1 teaspoon crushed dried herbs or 1/2 teaspoon ground herbs for each tablespoon fresh.

When you're out of ...

SPOON, FOR STIRRING JAM (or other easily burned mixtures)

Use a square-bladed spatula or pancake turner. Covers more area on the bottom of the pan, and gets in the "corners" where sides meet bottoms.

SUGAR, BROWN

Mix 1 to 2 tablespoons molasses into 1 cup granulated sugar.

OR:
If you're out of molasses — just substitute white sugar for brown —the taste won't be exactly the same, but it won't be displeasing.

SUGAR, BROWN SOFT

Place hardened brown sugar in a jar. Cover sugar with a wet paper towel (squeezed almost dry). Cover jar and leave overnight. Presto! Soft brown sugar.

OR:
If you need that hard sugar softened in a hurry, place brown sugar in an oven-proof pan or dish, and next to it, place a pan of very hot water. Close the oven door and let the steam take over.

OR:
To be sure the partially-used package of brown sugar doesn't have a chance to get hard, put a slice of bread into the box and close tightly.

When you're out of ...

SUGAR, FOR CANNING OR FREEZING FRUIT

SS▶ If you've a diabetic in the family, or just want to cut down on the calories in the syrup used in canning, try substituting fruit juices. Diabetics (as my husband is) need to remember to include as part of the exchange whatever juice is used when the fruit is served.

Apple, grapefruit, orange, pineapple and white grape juice may be used with peaches, pears, plums, apricots, etc. There is a slight reminder of the juice used, but the altered taste is pleasing. Just use the juice as you would sugar syrup, and process in a water bath as usual.

While fruit retain their texture better when frozen with some sugar, it is still possible to freeze them without sweetening. Darkening of peaches may be prevented by packing them in water containing ascorbic acid (one tablespoon of ascorbic acid crystals to one quart of water).

Berries may be frozen by placing them in a single layer on a cookie sheet, after washing in cold water. Or freeze fruit first, then wash. After the berries are frozen, put in plastic freezer bags or boxes. They will stay separate, so you can pour out and use what you need. Whether serving berries or fruits, thaw just until a few ice crystals remain, for better texture.

SUGAR FOR TEA

Try adding one teaspoon of your favorite orange-flavored drink powder to a hot cup of tea. Stir with a cinnamon stick. Now you have some of that new delightful cinnamon-orange tea. 'Tis much less costly than buying the same flavor in a tea bag!

SUGAR, POWDERED, ENOUGH

Frustrated when you've put too much milk in a butter-cream frosting, and you've used up all the powdered sugar? Add a bit of flour for spreading consistency. Cornstarch will work, also.

These hints make the frosting a little less sweet, which pleases some palates.

SUGAR, POWDERED

Put 1 cup granulated sugar and 2 tablespoons cornstarch in blender on medium low for about 45 seconds. Turn off and leave off for 2 or 3 minutes to let the "dust storm" subside, then turn on. Repeat 3 or 4 times. Don't take off the lid until the powder settles. Frostings are not quite as smooth when this is used in lieu of that commercially powdered.

OR:

If you just want to frost a cake, try this light and fluffy frosting aptly named:

ECONOMICAL FROSTING

4 T flour	1/2 c shortening
1 c milk	1 c sugar
1/4 c margarine	2 t vanilla

In a saucepan, mix flour with a little milk to make a paste, then add rest of milk and cook until thick. In a small mixer bowl, cream together margarine, shortening, sugar and vanilla until fluffy. Add cooled flour and milk mixture, and beat about two minutes.

Add 1 to 2 T cocoa for chocolate frosting.

This has a whipped cream texture and can also be used as a topping for puddings and pies.

SUGAR, WHITE

Use brown sugar as a substitute. This will add a faint molasses taste. You may want to add 1/4 t soda.

OR:

Try corn syrup, but reduce liquid called for in recipe by 1/4 cup per cup of sugar.

OR:

Use honey, and reduce liquid by 1/4 cup. Also, since honey is sweeter, 3/4 cup honey may replace 1 cup sugar.

OR:

Replace the sugar called for in cakes, muffins, cookies, etc., with an equal amount of jam. Not quite so sweet but will have a fruity taste.

OR:

While this recipe does not contain any refined sugar — anyone counting calories, or those on a diabetic diet should remember there is a lot of natural sugar in the apples and apple juice.

SS LC▶ SUGARLESS APPLE PIE

1 can (12 oz.) frozen apple juice concentrate, unsweetened
3 T cornstarch   1/2 t salt
1 t cinnamon   5 large, sweet apples, sliced

Combine cornstarch, frozen juice concentrate (undiluted), and cinnamon in a large pan. Heat until thickened. Add apples and simmer until apples are partially cooked. Pour into unbaked 9 or 10 inch pie shell. Cover with top crust, or with the following.

SS▶ SPECIAL CRUMB CRUST

1/2 c brown sugar   1/2 t cinnamon
   or brown sugar substitute   1/4 c chopped nuts
3/4 c whole wheat flour   1/3 c butter or margarine

Combine dry ingredients. Cut in butter or margarine. Sprinkle over top of pie before baking. Bake at 350° for 45 minutes.

When you're out of ...

SYRUP

Make your own in almost no time at all.

THREE-MINUTE SYRUP

1 c white sugar   1 c water
1 c brown sugar   1/2 t vanilla

Combine sugar and water in a saucepan. Boil until the sugar dissolves (about three minutes). Add vanilla. A new, fresh taste.
You can add a teaspoon of maple flavoring, if desired.

When you're out of ...

TENDERIZER FOR MEAT

Rub steak or chops with vinegar. Allow to stand two or three hours.

THE HOUSE

When you have to be gone, but want to come home to something scrumptious — here's a most unusual, but most delicious way of fixing roast beef.

CLOSED-DOOR ROAST BEEF

Preheat oven to 375°. Have roast at room temperature, salt and pepper and place in a shallow roasting pan. (Putting it on a rack browns the underside, but dries up the pan drippings so that it's hard to make gravy.) Roast for one hour, then turn OFF the oven, BUT DON'T OPEN THE OVEN DOOR! Leave in the oven for three hours — with the oven door CLOSED. (Open the door and the heat escapes, which spoils the whole process.) You can leave it in a bit longer than the three hours if necessary, and about 20 minutes before you are ready to serve, turn on the oven to 300° to heat it up.

This works with any size beef roast — from 2 1/2 to 10 pounds, and any kind — rolled boneless chuck, bone-in chuck, bottom round and sirloin tip. You can even use a frozen-solid roast — just add 1/2 hour to the original oven-on time.

When you're out of ...

TIME

No time for that elaborate decoration you'd planned for a special birthday cake? Use a plain icing and decorate with flowers cut from marshamallows or gumdrops. (Be sure to dampen scissors while cutting.)

OR:
Can't take the kids to town for their favorite drink? Try:

SS LC▶   ORANGE AUGUSTUS

> 1 can (6 oz.) frozen orange juice concentrate (undiluted)
> 1 c EACH milk and water   1 t vanilla
> 1/3 to 1/4 c sugar   8 ice cubes*
>   or sugar substitute

Combine all ingredients in a blender, and run at medium-high speed until you can no longer hear the ice rattling. Add 1/2 to 1 cup of yogurt for extra protein and creaminess. Serves 4 delighted people.
*Ice makers usually make smaller cubes, so you'll need 16.

OR:
Out of time as well as meat? Adding some extra ingredients gives canned pork and beans a long-baked flavor.

"HOMESTYLE" BAKED BEANS

> 1 (32 oz.) can pork and beans   4 slices bacon
> 2 T finely chopped onion   4 T brown sugar
> 1 to 2 T vinegar

Combine ingredients in baking pan; top with bacon and bake 20 minutes in 425° oven.

Micro≈ Combine ingredients in a shallow baking pan and cook 10 minutes, stirring once. Sprinkle with crisped, crumbled bacon. (See page 87 for microwaving the bacon.)

OR:

SPEEDY BAKED BEANS

3 or 4 cups cooked
navy beans
or 1 (No. 2 1/2 can)
pork and beans
1 c pineapple chunks
1 medium onion, chopped

1/4 c catsup
4 or 5 T brown sugar
2 T lemon juice
Prepared mustard to taste
4 slices bacon

Mix all ingredients together except bacon, and place in 9x13-inch baking dish. Place bacon strips on top and bake in 350° oven for about 45 minutes.

(You can use 1/2 cup pineapple juice for the chunks; vinegar for lemon juice; or tomato sauce for catsup.

Micro≈ Follow directions for "Homestyle Baked Beans", page 76.

OR:

An EASY, tasty change from Hollandaise on Eggs Benedict and works well on recipes calling for the more complicated Sauce Mornay.

CHICO GOURMET SAUCE

1/2 lb. Velveeta (or any brand pasteurized process cheese)
1/4 c milk   1/2 t onion powder

Cut cheese into cubes and heat with milk in saucepan over low heat, stirring until sauce is smooth. Add onion powder and mix well. Makes one cup sauce. Serve warm over omelettes, vegetables or filled crepes.

If you want to serve it over small boiling onions, omit the onion powder and season with herbs such as basil, thyme, mace, etc. Do not use herb *salts* —cheese is salty enough.

Micro≈ Put milk and cubed cheese into 2-cup glass measure. Micro 2 or 3 minutes until cheese is melted, stirring once or twice.

BONUS HINT: When cold, the sauce hardens to spreading consistency and may be jazzed up with chili or jalapeno peppers, while still warm and easy to stir. Cover while cooling to prevent "crusting". A super dip for fresh veggies, pretzels, or chips; and a great spread on crackers.

OR:

Here's a way to get beautifully browned chicken without taking the time to fry it. If you remove the skin, you will have a more delicious chicken, and will have reduced the fat and calorie intake even more.

LF▶   SOY SAUCE CHICKEN

Pour about 1/2 cup soy sauce and 1/2 cup water into an electric frying pan. Arrange chicken pieces one layer deep. Cover and simmer gently for 1/2 hour, then turn pieces to brown other side. (May need to add a bit more soy sauce and water.) Simmer for another half hour.

Adding a 1/2 teaspoon of ground ginger, a dash of garlic salt, and about a tablespoon of sugar will give the finished chicken a teriyaki flavor.

Serve with rice or boiled noodles, or see FAKE CHINESE NOODLES, p. 61.

Micro≈ Follow all directions, except arrange chicken in 10-inch pie plate, with meatier pieces on the outer edge. Micro for 6 to 8 minutes, turn over and micro another 5 or 6 minutes.

OR:

STIR-FRY SANDWICH FILLING

Need a fast hot sandwich and have an uncooked roast in the refrigerator? Cut into very thin slices, marinate for a few minutes in 1/2 cup soy sauce mixed with 1/2 teaspoon each of ginger and garlic salt. Remove meat from marinade and stir-fry quickly in small amount of oil or margarine. Serve between two slices of toasted bread.

TOMATO SAUCE

A pint jar (or 16-ounce can) of tomatoes processed in the blender with your favorite seasonings will produce an acceptable substitute.

OR:

Use tomato juice. It will thicken if you leave off the lid and let the water simmer away while you're cooking it with the onions, meat and flavorings.

TOMATO SAUCE, FOR MEATLOAF

Use any kind of cream soup — diluted with 1/2 soup-can of water as a tasty replacement for tomato sauce or catsup. If you have two cans of the same kind of soup, use the extra can diluted with just 1/4 can of water, and use as gravy over the meatloaf.

When you're out of ...

TORTILLA CHIPS

The secret to making these crunchy chips is in spreading the batter THIN.

HOMEMADE CORN CHIPS

1 c water	1 c yellow cornmeal
2 T butter or margarine	1/2 t salt

Bring water, margarine and salt to a boil. Remove from heat and stir in cornmeal gradually, stirring until thick and smooth. Place dough on a greased cookie sheet, and with wet hands, press very thinly over entire cookie sheet, or use a dampened rolling pin to help you get the mixture thin and even. If your cookie sheet is small, divide into two batches.

Bake in 400° oven for 15 to 20 minutes or until lightly brown. When cool, loosen with a spatula, break into large pieces, and turn over on a cake-drying rack. If the center portion seems moist, return to oven (upside down) on cookie sheet and continue crisping for a few more minutes.

For TACO-FLAVORED TORILLA CHIPS add about three teaspoons hot taco sauce to water, butter and salt mixture. A half teaspoon of chili sauce may be added also for a still spicier taste.

VANILLA

Try 1/4 teaspoon of maple flavoring.

VEAL

When turkey breasts are on sale you might like to try:

"VEAL" PICATTE SURPRISE

1 lb. raw turkey breast	Salt and pepper
Flour	1 T finely minced parsley
1/4 c butter	Juice of 1 lemon

Cut the raw turkey breast in 1/4-inch-thick slices. Pound between wax paper to about 1/8-inch. Coat with flour. Heat butter until sizzling. Add turkey slices and brown quickly on both sides. Place on hot platter.

Stir salt, pepper and lemon juice in the pan and pour over the slices. Sprinkle with parsley.

OR:

A delicious taste-alike for Veal Parmesan that won't break your budget is this version using ground turkey.

TURKEY PARMESAN

1 lb. ground turkey	1/2 t each oregano and basil
3/4 c bread crumbs	(dried leaves)
2 T vegetable oil	8 slices Monterey Jack cheese
1 15-oz. can tomato sauce	1/2 c grated Parmesan cheese

Shape turkey into four 1/2-inch thick oval patties. Dip into bread crumbs. Lightly brown in pre-heated oil over moderate heat, about 2 or 3 minutes. Arrange patties in oblong baking dish, cover each with 2 slices of Jack cheese, pour tomato sauce over, and sprinkle with Parmesan. Bake in 400° oven about 10 to 15 minutes.

When you're out of ...

VEGETABLES, FRESH

One 16-ounce can vegetables, drained or 2 cups frozen loose-pack vegetables can be substituted for 2 cups of cooked fresh vegetables.

1 10 oz. package of frozen vegetables, or 1 1/4 cups loose-pack equals 1 1/4 cups fresh cooked.

VEGETABLE JUICE COCKTAIL

Buy a 48 ounce can of plain tomato juice. Put into pitcher and add 1 teaspoon celery salt, 1/2 teaspoon onion salt, 1/2 teaspoon garlic powder, 1 teaspoon sugar. Stir thoroughly.

VINEGAR

Use lemon juice — same measurements.

WATER CHESTNUTS

Jicamas add the same crunchy goodness to Chinese cooking. Mild radishes may also be used.

When you're out of ...

WAX PAPER

Liners from cereal boxes are excellent for lining baking pans. They are heavier than regular wax paper (and free!)

WHIPPED TOPPING

Into the white of an egg, slice two ripe bananas and beat until stiff and bananas are dissolved.

OR:
Beat the white of an egg until frothy, beat in 2 or 3 T sugar, then scrape an apple into mixture and continue beating until stiff. Must be used immediately or apple starts to brown.

OR:
Melt marshmallows, cool and beat with one egg white until stiff.

OR:
For flavored topping or fluffy cake frosting beat together 1 egg white and 1/2 cup jelly.

OR:
See Economical Frosting, page 33.

When you're out of ...

WINE OR OTHER ALCOHOLIC BEVERAGES, FOR COOKING

These substitutes will give good results since the alternates are compatible with the same foods as the alcoholic beverages they replace.

FOR SOUPS OR ENTREES

Dry red wine

Beef broth, tomato juice, diluted cider vinegar, liquid from canned mushrooms

Dry white wine

Chicken broth, ginger ale, white grape juice, diluted cider vinegar, liquid from canned mushrooms

FOR CHEESE DISHES (Fondue or Rarebit)

Beer or ale

Chicken broth, white grape juice, ginger ale

IN DESSERTS

Brandy	Apple cider, peach or apricot syrup
Burgundy, red	Grape juice
Burgundy, white	White grape juice
Champagne	Ginger ale
Claret	Grape or currant juice or syrup, cherry cider
Cognac	Juice of peaches, apricots or pears
Cointreau	Orange juice or frozen orange juice concentrate
Creme de menthe	Spearmint extract or oil of spearmint diluted with a little water; grapefruit juice
Kirsch	Syrup or juice of black cherries, raspberries, boysenberries, currants, or grape or cherry cider
Sherry	Orange or pineapple juice
Rum	Pineapple juice or syrup plus almond extract

To cut sweetness of syrup, or acidity of vinegar — dilute one-fourth to one-half with water. Also, it's good to know that flavoring extracts from health food stores have no alcohol content. Extra: If you want to try a flaming dessert — soak a sugar cube briefly in lemon extract, light and use in any flambé.

Try out a wine substitute in this recipe

CHICKEN BAKED IN WINE

1 2 1/2-3 lb. broiler-fryer	1/2 t curry powder
Seasoned salt	2 T cornstarch
2 T vinegar*	1/4 c water
2 T water*	1 4 oz. can mushrooms,
1 t sugar*	drained (optional)
1 c chicken broth	6 water chestnuts,
1 t instant minced onion	sliced (optional)

Cut chicken in serving pieces. Sprinkle lightly on both sides with seasoned salt. Place skin-side-down in baking dish. Mix together vinegar, water, sugar, chicken broth, onion and curry powder. Cover and bake at 350° for 30 minutes.

Uncover and turn chicken pieces and continue to bake 30 minutes more. Remove chicken from pan and skim off any fat from the meat juices. Mix the 2 tablespoons of cornstarch with 1/4 cup water, and stir into meat juices. Add mushrooms and water chestnuts, if used. Cook over low heat, stirring constantly until sauce is thickened. Spoon over chicken before serving. Serves 4 to 6.

*These may be replaced with 1/4 cup sherry.

Micro≈ Increase cornstarch to 3 T and water to 1/3 cup, and stir together. Place chicken and all other ingredients in 3 or 4 quart baking dish. Stir in cornstarch and water. Add mushrooms and water chestnuts and micro for 16 to 20 minutes.

OR:

PORTUGUESE POT ROAST

1 7-bone roast (3 or 4 lbs.)
1 c diced celery, including tops
1/2 lb. sliced fresh mushrooms, or 1 (4 oz.) can
1 can tomatoes
1/2 c onions
1/2 c sherry (or 1/4 c vinegar and 1/4 c water)

Place roast in large roasting pan or casserole; arrange other ingredients over and around roast. Cover with aluminum foil, or tight-fitting lid. Bake at 350° for two hours.

Remove roast to hot platter; then mix 2 to 3 tablespoons cornstarch with about 1/4 cup cold water, and stir into pan juices, cooking gently until thickened.

To serve, slice roast and pour gravy and vegetables over.

When you're out of ...

YEAST FOR BREAD

Try this fast one.

BEER BREAD

3 cups self-rising flour   1 12-ounce can of beer
3 T sugar

Mix together ingredients. Put into one large greased bread-loaf pan (about 4 1/2 x 9 1/2) or two smaller ones. Let rise 10 minutes. Put in preheated 375° oven for 50 to 60 minutes. Keep an eye on the bread while it's baking — oven times will vary, depending on the brand of the beer, as well as the texture and taste.
No self-rising flour?
Add 6 t baking powder and 1 1/2 t salt to 3 cups of regular flour.

OR:
Give your Beer Bread a sour-dough taste by using 8 ounces of beer with 4 ounces of yogurt, and omitting the sugar. Follow the same directions for regular beer bread.
BONUS HINT: Wrap either of these breads immediately after removing from the oven in a plastic bag (bread wrappers do nicely) to prevent the crust from getting crumbly.

OR:
A▶   DUBLIN SODA BREAD

When we discovered that my daughter was allergic to yeast we were delighted to find this recipe for Soda Bread. It has a texture very similar to coarse wheat bread, and when made with half whole wheat flour is extra nutritious.

4 c flour   1/8 t cardamon or
(all white or half whole wheat)   coriander (optional)
1 t salt   1/4 c margarine
3 t baking soda   1 egg
1 t soda   1 3/4 c buttermilk
1/4 c sugar (optional)

Combine dry ingredients in a large bowl. Cut in margarine with a pastry blender or two knives until crumbly. Add the slightly beaten egg to the buttermilk, then stir into dry ingredients until well blended. Knead 2 or 3 minutes on a floured board.

84

Divide dough in half and shape each into a round ball. Press each loaf into an 8-inch cake or pie pan until dough fills pan. Cut a 1/2 inch deep cross in the middle of each loaf with a sharp knife. Bake for 35 to 40 minutes in a 375° oven. 2 loaves.

Two cups raisins or currants may be added to the above recipe. It's best to include the sugar, and leave out the spice if you do. Dates are a tasty addition to the whole wheat version. In both cases, mix the fruit with the dry ingredients before combining with the liquid.

When you're out of ...

YEAST FOR PIZZA DOUGH

Try these different "bottoms".

Use flour tortillas, brushing both sides lightly with salad oil, making sure edges are oiled. When covered with your favorite "toppings" bake 7 to 10 minutes in 475° oven.

OR:
Use hamburger buns, or those bread heels you've been saving.

OR:
Split English Muffins (sour dough or sweet).

OR:
Slice French Bread lengthwise. If sliced in thirds, toast the middle section.

Here's a good topping for any of the above bottoms.

HAMBURGER PIZZA

1/2 lb. ground beef (or any other meat of your choice)	
1/8 t pepper	1/4 t oregano
3/4 t salt	1/8 c green onion or chives,
1/4 c parmesan cheese	minced
2/3 c tomato paste	14 slices tomatoes,
1/4 c chopped olives	8 slices American cheese

Saute meat until brown. Remove from heat and add rest of ingredients except tomatoes and American cheese. Spread hamburger mixture on pizza bottom. Lay sliced tomatoes on top and cover with American cheese. Bake at 400° for 15 minutes.

MICRO FACTS

≈ **The microwave book** that came with your oven is your best source of information. However, depending on when you got your current oven, there may be newer developments — and all microwave cookbooks are not created equal. So here are a few facts that might be helpful, and some specific hints on the next page.

≈ **Since microwave energy** does not penetrate more than an inch or so into food, donut-shaped cookware is the most practical. Microwave-safe bundt pans and ring molds are best for baking cakes and quick breads, or meat loaves and casseroles.

≈ **The next best shape** is round — to avoid having to cover the corners of rectangular pans with aluminum foil to avoid overcooking. (You can change round to donut by placing a two-inch water glass in the middle of a round pie plate or glass casserole.)

≈ **Handiest cookware** for other kinds of cooking are 2-, 4- and 6-cup heat proof glass measures. You can melt things ... cook up sauces ... scald milk (careful not to boil — it foams over quickly) ... heat up soups ... boil water (about 3 minutes a cup) ... heat up syrup (about 30 seconds).

≈ **If your oven** does not have a turn table, you will have to rotate a quarter turn halfway through the cooking time. Even with a rotating oven, stirrable food must be stirred halfway through the cooking time to bring the middle portion to the edges where the energy can reach it. Non-stirrables need a resting time, to let the heat penetrate to the middle. And their resting needs to be done on a heat proof flat surface such as a cutting board to keep the heat from escaping.

≈ **Wax paper** is one of the best covers. If you use plastic be sure to turn back an edge for venting the steam, also plastic may melt if exposed to fats or sugars.

≈ **Always remember** that bowls, jars, casseroles get HOT — the heat transfers from the hot food. Keep pot holders handy.

≈ **When reheating** in a microwave, think *seconds* not *minutes*. Small pieces of food dehydrate easily and it's impossible to restore them.

≈ **Microwave equipment** which may prove helpful include a wind-up turntable for non-revolving ovens, a browning dish for giving meats the finished color we're used to, a microwave rack to elevate food so that moisture is not trapped underneath, a microwave popcorn maker.

MICRO HINTS

≈ **Artichokes** do best one at a time. Rinse well, trim stems, place in a small plastic bag, stand upright in oven and microwave about 5 minutes for medium, 8 minutes for extra large. Let set in bag a few minutes before serving.

≈ **Bacon** stays crisp and fat-free without a browning pan if cooked this way. Spread out a paper towel or two on a plate or platter, then scrunch the paper toward you, making accordian pleats. Place the bacon on top and cover with another paper towel. Cook about 1 minute per slice.

≈ **Baked potatoes** dehydrate quickly, so check often, by squeezing gently with a potholdered hand. They should give, but still feel firm. Start with potatoes as close to the same size as possible. Wash, but do not dry. Pierce with a fork, and place in oven on a paper towel in "spoke" formation. Allow about 3 minutes per potato. Check and turn over at half the cooking time, moving from the wet spot on the towel to a dry one. Remove and let rest at least 3 more minutes, covered.

≈ **Bread** tends to get rubbery or soggy. You can avoid the former by heating for about 30 seconds at half power, and eliminate the latter by wrapping the sandwich or slice of bread in a paper towel.

≈ **Corn on the cob** is super when you remove all but 2 layers of husks, retaining the silk. The husks and silk are your "cooking bag". Micro for 2 or 3 minutes per ear. Remove wrappings carefully — you'll need pot holders.

≈ **For muffins**, if you have no micro-safe pan, cut paper drinking cubs (*not* plastic foam) about 1 1/2 to 2 inches. Spray with vegetable coating or line with fluted paper baking cups and fill 1/2 full. You'll have hot muffins ready in about 3/4 to 1 minute per muffin! This works for cupcakes also.

≈ **Microwaved vegetables** retain color, nutrients and flavor. An easy way to cook up to 6 servings of cut-up veggies: Use the plastic bags you bought them in, lightly twisting closed, and flattening out in the oven. Cook for 3 to 4 minutes for crisp tender. Do not cook for more than 5 or 6 minutes since these thin bags cannot stand the heat for too long. Remove from oven and let sit for a few minutes to continue cooking. Be careful when opening, the steam is HOT!

≈ **Strawberries** can be sliced and mashed, then sprinkled with sugar to taste and cooked for about 3 minutes (stirring each minute to distribute the sugar) to make a fresh-tasting spread for french toast, waffles, pancakes or spooned over ice cream. This keeps in the refrigerator for a week or two. Any other berry may be used — just wash and crush. Glass measuring cups make good utensils for this.

MICRO HINTS (cont)

≈ **Soften** hard ice cream. Microwave at medium low power for 15 to 30 seconds for one pint, 30 to 45 for a quart, and 45 seconds to one minute for a half-gallon.

≈ **Soften** butter or margarine — at low power for one minute.

≈ **Soften** cream cheese. One 8-ounce package will take 2 to 2 1/2 minutes at medium low power. A 3-ounce package will soften in 1 1/2 to 2 minutes.

≈ **Soften** jello that set up too hard while you were chilling it to become slightly thickened. Heat at 50% power for 10 to 20 seconds. When about an inch has melted around the outside you can stir it into the middle for the syrupy texture you need.

≈ **Thaw** frozen orange juice for easier mixing. Remove the top metal lid and then microwave on high power for 30 seconds for 6 ounces. It will take about 45 seconds for 12 ounces.

≈ **Dissolve** gelatin. Measure liquid in a large glass measuring cup, add gelatin and heat for about 3 minutes, stirring each minute, until gelatin is dissolved.

≈ **Re-crisp** potato or corn chips that have gone limp — or other snacks such as crackers. Put on a microwave proof plate and heat for about 30 to 45 seconds. Let stand for 1 minute to crisp. Refresh dry cereal the same way.

≈ **Melt** marshmallow creme. It takes 35-40 seconds on high to melt half of a 7-ounce jar.

≈ **Melt** butter, margarine, shortening. Any time a recipe calls for one of these to be melted and then combined with sugar, chocolate, etc. just put the it in a large glass measuring cup, place in the micro and zap for about 10 seconds — depending on the quantity. When melted, add the other ingredients, stir and heat for another 20 to 30 seconds.

≈ **Blanch, then toast** almonds. Put 1 cup almonds in a two cup measure. Cover with water, then heat until boiling — about 2 1/2 to 3 minutes. Pour out the hot water, and rinse with cool, then pop off the skins. Layer on a glass pie plate and heat on high 1 to 2 minutes. Stir halfway through (to bring the middles to the outside), then toast until golden brown. If a few on the edges happen to turn almost black — not to worry. Your friends will think they're eating smoked almonds!

EQUIVALENTS

VEGETABLES, FRUITS

Apples, 1 pound .... 2 large or 3 medium
2 1/2 to 3 cups sliced
Bananas, 1 pound .... 3 or 4 medium
2 1/2 cups sliced
2 cups mashed
Beans, 1 pound, dried .... 1 1/2 to 2 cups
5 to 6 cups, cooked
Cabbage, 1 pound .... 1 medium
4 cups shredded, raw
2 cups cooked
Carrots, 1 pound .... 6 to 7 medium
4 cups shredded or grated
3 cups cooked
Celery, 1 stalk .... 1/3 cup, diced
Dates, 1 pound .... 2 1/4 cups whole
1 1/2 - 2 cups pitted, chopped
Figs, 1 pound .... 2 2/3 cups, peeled, chopped
Green pepper, 1 medium .... 1 cup diced
Mushrooms   1 pound .... 5 cups sliced
Lemon .... 2 to 3 Tbsp. juice
Onion, 1 medium .... 1 1/4 cup, chopped
Orange, 1 medium .... 1/3 to 1/2 cup juice
1 to 2 Tbsp. grated peel
Peaches, 1 pound .... 4 medium
2 cups sliced, peeled
Peas, 1 pound in pod .... 1 cup shelled
Potatoes, 1 pound .... 3 medium
2 1/2 cups cooked, diced
1 3/4 cup, mashed
Prunes, 1 pound .... 2 1/4 cup pitted
3 cups, cooked
Raisins, 1 pound .... 2 to 2 1/2 cups, uncooked
Tomatoes, 1 pound .... 2 to 3 medium
1 8-ounce can
1 cup chopped

OTHER FOODSTUFFS

Baking chocolate, 1 square .... 1 ounce
Butter, 1 pound .... 2 cups, 4 sticks
    1/2 pound .... 1 cup, 2 sticks
    1/4 pound .... 1/2 cup, 1 stick
    1/2 stick .... 4 Tbsp. or 1/4 cup
Cheese, 1/4 pound, (4 ounces) .... 3/4 cup grated
    1 cup shredded
Cheese, Cream 3 oz. .... 6 Tbsp.
    1/2 lb. .... 16 Tbsp. (1 cup)
Chicken, 3 1/2 lb. cooked .... 2 cups diced meat
Chocolate chips, 12 oz. .... 2 cups (see page 18)
Coffee, 1 lb. ground .... 80 Tablespoons
    (1 Tbsp. brews 1 cup)
Cornmeal, 1 pound .... 2 2/3 cups
Cream, for whipping, 1 cup .... 2 cups whipped
Crumb Count .... see page 11
Flour, 1 pound
    White .... 3 1/2 to 4 cups
    Cake .... 4 to 4 1/2 cups
    Wheat .... 3 cups, sifted
    Rye .... 4 cups
    Graham .... 3 1/2 to 3 3/4 cups
    Rice .... 2 cups
Gelatin 3 1/4 oz. pkg. (flavored) .... 1/2 cup
    1/4 oz. pkg. (unflavored) .... 1 Tbsp.
Honey, 1 pound .... 1 1/3 cup
Macaroni, 1 pound .... 8 to 9 cups, cooked
Margarine .... See butter
Marshmallows, large, 1 pound .... 64 marshmallows
    11 large .... 1 cup
    1 large .... 7 miniature
Noodles .... 6 to 8 cups cooked
Rice, 1 cup uncooked .... 2 cups, cooked
    1 pound .... 2 to 2 1/2 cups uncooked
Spaghetti, 1 pound .... 6 1/2 cups cooked
Sugar, 1 pound
    Granulated white .... 2 cups
    Powdered .... 3 1/2 to 4 cups
    Brown .... 2 1/4 cups, firmly packed
Tea, 1 pound .... 100 servings
Yogurt, 1 pound .... 3 1/4 cups

EQUIVALENTS (cont.)

NUTS

Almonds, 1 pound
  In the shell .... 1 to 1 1/2 cups nutmeats
  Shelled .... 3 1/2 cups
Peanuts
  In the shell .... 2 1/4 cups nutmeats
  Shelled .... 3 cups
Pecans, 1 pound
  In the shell .... 2 1/4 cups nutmeats
  Shelled .... 3 to 4 cups
Walnuts, 1 pound
  In the shell .... 1 1/2 cups nutmeats
  Shelled .... 4 cups

MEASUREMENTS

3 tsp. = 1 Tbsp.

4 Tbsp. =	1/4 cup	= 2 oz. =	1/8 pound*
8 Tbsp. =	1/2 cup	= 4 oz. =	1/4 pound*
16 Tbsp. =	1 cup	= 8 oz. =	1/2 pound*
2 Cups =	1 pint	= 16 oz. =	1 pound*
4 Cups =	1 quart	= 32 oz. =	2 pounds*

*Please Note: The old memory jogger, "A pint's a pound, the world around", applies to liquids of about the same density.

When it comes to dry ingredients it's a different story. Check out the equivalent volumes of flour and sugar, for example.

PROPORTIONS

Baking powder: 2 teaspoons to 1 cup of flour
Baking soda: 1/2 teaspoon to 1 cup of milk
                1/2 teaspoon to 1 cup of molasses
Gelatin: 1 Tablespoon to 2 cups of liquid.

POT POURRI OF BONUS HINTS

Many of the hints sent in would not fit a particular "out of", but were too helpful to leave out. So here they are — with no attempt to classify or put in any order.

To get walnut meats out whole — soak the nuts overnight in salt water. To save the half-shells — just pry them apart with a paring knife.

To keep the salt shaker dry and free-flowing during humid weather, keep a clear drinking glass turned upside down over the shaker.

To keep cottage cheese, yogurt, cream cheese, etc. fresh almost indefinitely, turn the carton upside down while storing. Be sure to tap the top before opening — to settle things down.

Used, crumpled aluminum foil makes a dandy scouring pad for pots or pans and for scraping dishes before placing in dishwasher.

Recipes that call for just one or two tablespoons of tomato paste often mean wasting most of a can. Just freeze the leftover paste on foil or waxed paper in tablespoonful-sized mounds. When frozen, store in a plastic bag or container for future use.

Instead of an ice-ring to float in a punch bowl — freeze whole (washed) lemons, limes and/or oranges and float them in the bowl.

For those of you who wear braces and can't eat popcorn (which you LOVE as much as the junior-high student who sent in this recipe), try this:
Melt 1/4 cup butter or margarine in a skillet over low heat. Add four cups of toasted ready-to-eat oat cereal (the kind shaped like little doughnuts). Cook and stir until well-coated and hot, about 2 or 3 minutes; then sprinkle with salt.
This really tastes just about the same as popcorn!

An old-fashioned, spring-type nut cracker is perfect for opening stubborn screw-type bottle caps.

Make your own "ice cream bars" by freezing any flavor of an instant (or cooked and cooled pudding). Molds can be purchased, or any cookie cutter without holes, can be used. Stick in a sucker stick and freeze. For "popsicles" freeze gelatin desserts in the same fashion.

Need to add crispness to a tuna or chicken salad, and you're fresh out of celery? A diced apple makes a good in-lieu-of.

No coffee cream, or creamer in the house? Blend 3 tablespoons real butter (not margarine), melted, with 3/4 cups milk.

Left over gelatin dessert can be recycled by placing the gelatin and an equal amount of vanilla ice cream in your blender. (The mixer can be used but it takes much longer.) Blend until the two are fluid, then pour quickly into serving dishes or parfait glasses, as it sets up fast. This dessert has the color of the original gelatin, which may be used even if you had fruit molded in it. Does not have to be kept in the freezer. You can pour it into a baked pie crust for a "cream" pie.

LC▶ Use potato flakes for thickening soups. Calorie-wise, potato flakes are 60 per 1/2 cup, compared to flour at 224 per 1/2 cup and cornstarch at 240.

Mix chocolate syrup with prepared whipped topping for a quick frosting.

This hint has nothing to do with homemaking or cooking, but since so many of you are mail order customers, I'd like to pass it along.
Always put the address of the company you're ordering from on the back of your check (on the bottom — opposite the endorsement spot.) That way, if your check is cleared, and no merchandise received, you have a permanent record of where your order was sent, and a chance to send an inquiry.

Leftover stuffing? Form into patties (add a little water if stuffing seems to dry.) Sizzle in enough margarine to just cover the bottom of a frying pan until golden on both sides. Serve with gravy, or one recipe of GWEN'S SOUP MIX (page 24).

Here's a delicious way of using leftover baked potatoes.
Slice into 1/4 inch pieces — DO NOT PEEL! Frizzle in margarine, browning both sides quickly. Salt and pepper. Serve with hot catsup, or try grated sharp cheddar cheese to melt on the hot slices.

No "undrafty" places for raising bread dough?
Set bread dough in lightly covered bowl on middle rack of oven. Place a pan of boiling water on floor of oven. You don't have to turn on oven. (Bonus: Steam loosens oven spatters for easy cleaning.)

For a miniature ice-bag — keep a few used tea bags in the freezer. Handy for young children, or for an adult's small nick or cut.

When you're using a cookbook that doesn't stay flat when opened ... place an 8x8 or 9x9-inch square glass baking pan over the pages. This keeps the book flat and the pages stay clean.

If you don't want to cut up a large sheet of paper for a tiny box like a jewelry box, use aluminum foil. A pretty glitter for Christmas presents.

LC▶ Cut calories, add protein and calcium; and stretch the cost of commercially prepared bottled salad dressings by adding one cup of plain yogurt to an 8 ounce bottle. Enhances the flavor and adds creaminess.

An easy way to achieve the taste of those yummy twice-baked potatoes. Instead of having to bake the potatoes, scrape out the insides, stir in the goodies, and then replace them in the baked shell — just make MASHED POTATO CASSEROLE.
To each 2 1/2 to 3 cups of leftover mashed potatoes, blend in one cup of sour cream, and about three or four chopped green onions. Put into greased casserole, top with shredded cheese and bake at 350° until hot and cheese is melted (about 15 minutes). Top with bacon bits, if desired.

Colorless nail-polish makes a good emergency glue for small items like stamps, recipe clippings, etc. Also red nail polish is great when some small item needs a coat of red — such as house numbers; names on kids' boots or on their lunch boxes.

If none of your frying pans has a heat-proof handle, you can wrap the handle completely with aluminum foil to make it oven-proof.

Enhance the flavor of prepared cookie or muffin mixes by replacing with vanilla all or part of the liquid called for in the recipe. For example, if the recipe requires 1/4 cup milk, use 2 tablespoons vanilla and 2 tablespoons milk. In biscuit or pancake mixes, measure 2 tablespoons vanilla in the measuring cup, then finish with milk or water.

Sneak needed fiber into the family's diet by adding bran, granola, or other high-fiber cereal to cookie or muffin recipes in place of nuts.

Anyone needing to use a salt substitute knows that a little is fine but that adding too much turns everything bitter. Add 5 teaspoons paprika to 4 tablespoons salt substitute to turn the seasoning pink. This makes the "un-salt" more visible so you won't over-do it.
If you want to add a bit more pungent flavor — along with the paprika, mix in 2 teaspoons EACH garlic **powder and onion powder***.
*Be sure to use POWDER not SALT!

Here's a low-cal mini pie crust to use with sugar-free pie fillings. Melt 1 to 2 tablespoons margarine in the pie plate (can do it in the microwave in about 30 seconds). Stir in 16 square graham crackers, crushed, and press firmly just into bottom of the pie pan. Best to refrigerate before adding filling.

Leftover meatloaf, crumbled, is practically a ready-made stuffing for bell peppers. Can add some cooked rice or potatoes for an extender.

When you're watching fat and cholesterol intake — frozen tofu, grated, is a good extender for hamburger or ground turkey in chili, tacos, enchiladas, or meatloaf. Freezing the soy product changes the texture to more closely resemble ground meat.

SUPER BONUS HINT:

Would you like to learn how to save electricity by harnessing the energy from the sun for cooking, baking and canning? Write to:
Solar Box Cookers International
1724 Eleventh Street, Dept T
Sacramento, CA 95814   (916) 444-6616
This organization has information about ordering insulated cardboard cookers that bake bread, cakes and muffins; cook meat, vegetables, casseroles; and do a superb job of making the canning of fruits and tomatoes a cool, easy task. They also have instructions for making your own energy-saving cooker using cardboard boxes, aluminum foil and a sheet of glass. Do send a legal-size, stamped, self-addressed envelope since this is a non-profit organization.

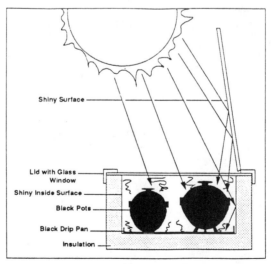

Cross section of a Solar Box Cooker

INDEX OF SPECIAL RECIPES

Our readers with allergies have made us aware of these special recipes that have helped them. These are marked with A▶. But do take care. When you're out of eggs, you can substitute mayonnaise for a cake — but not if you're allergic to them, because mayonnaise has eggs in it. The same with the Beer Bread — there is yeast in beer, so this recipe cannot be used if you're allergic to yeast.

When you'd like to cut down on animal protein try alternative proteins, designated AP▶ next to the recipe title, or by a hint.

Looking for recipes that are low calorie, low fat or that use sugar substitutes? Look for LC▶ (low calorie), LF▶ (low fat) or SS▶ (sugar substitute).

RECIPE INDEX

* Includes Microwave Directions

* Includes Microwave Directions

A FINAL WORD ...

It has been nearly a decade since our first little booklet, "THIS FOR THAT", came off the press. Its popularity took it to every state in the union, many Canadian Provinces, to Mexico and even overseas where military families and missionaries found its substitutions and alternative recipes essential.

Thanks to the enthusiastic response to our request for new "out of's" we were able to expand to the larger "WHEN YOU'RE OUT OF ..." from which this edition comes — renamed "THIS FOR THAT". (A mini-survey proved that most people preferred the original name.)

To make room for the addition of microwave directions we had to eliminate the names of donors, but do want to acknowledge our indebtedness to these "suggesters" and let them know that their names remain in our files and in our hearts.

In keeping with this tradition, we would like to invite all of our readers to send in suggestions — whether they be new items for the "in lieu of" category, or the microwave conversions mentioned at the front of the book. If your suggestion is used, you will receive a free copy of the book in which it appears.

Suggestions ... and orders may be sent to:

THIS 'N THAT PRESS
P.O. Box 504
Galt, California 95632

We are looking forward to hearing from you. Happy Cooking!

Meryl Nelson
Shirley Sing
Frances Thoman

Your Own Notes ...